M000289293

App
Design
Apprentice

By Prateek Prasad

App Design Apprentice

By Prateek Prasad

Copyright ©2020 Razeware LLC.

ISBN: 978-1-950325-20-7

Dedications

"In loving memory of my grandfather."

— Prateek Prasad

About the Authors

 **Prateek Prasad** is an engineer and a self taught designer. He started writing mobile apps when he was in high school and has a soft spot for beautifully designed products. He is a massive comic book nerd (which might have even influenced this book a little). He spends his free time listening and playing music or thinking about outer space.

About the Editors

 **Luke Freeman** is a tech editor for this book and also the Design Lead at raywenderlich.com. Luke specializes in visual design, color, typography and user experience design. When he's not designing and developing you can find him cooking pasta, walking his hound Hunter, watching Arsenal and playing football!

 **Lea Marolt Sonnenschein** is a tech editor for this book. Lea spent three years in New York, working on the iOS application for Rent the Runway and teaching Swift at General Assembly. Now, she's getting a masters in Innovation Design Engineering in London, and spends most of her time playing with sensors and microcontrollers. She writes articles focused on design and usability for raywenderlich.com, and is the author of one of the most popular video courses on the site, Reproducing Popular iOS Controls.

 **Sandra Grauschopf** is the Editing Team Lead at raywenderlich.com. She's an experienced writer, editor, and content manager who loves to explore the world with a book in her hand.

Matthew Morey is the final pass editor for this book. Matthew is an engineer, developer, hacker, creator, and tinkerer. As an active member of the mobile community and head of technology at Valtech he has led numerous successful mobile projects worldwide. He's the creator of Buoy Explorer, a marine conditions app for water sports enthusiast, and Wrist Presenter, an app that lets you control presentations wirelessly with your smart watch. When not developing apps he enjoys traveling, snowboarding, and surfing.

About the Artist

Vicki Wenderlich is the designer and artist of the cover of this book. She is Ray's wife and business partner. She is a digital artist who creates illustrations, game art and a lot of other art or design work for the tutorials and books on raywenderlich.com. When she's not making art, she loves hiking, a good glass of wine and attempting to create the perfect cheese plate.

Table of Contents

Book License

By purchasing *App Design Apprentice*, you have the following license:

Before You Begin

This section tells you a few things you need to know before you get started, such as what you'll need for hardware and software, where to find the project files for this book, and more.

What You Need

To follow along with this book, you'll need the following:

- A Mac running **El Capitan** (10.11) or later, or a Windows machine running **Windows 8** or later in a 64-bit environment.

- An iPhone, iPad or iPod touch running **iOS 10.0** or later, or an Android device running **Android 7.0** or later.

- At least build **85 of Figma**. While learning how to use Figma is an important part of this book, the most important thing to come away with is an understanding of the foundational design principles that you can leverage with any version of Figma or any tool.

Where to download the materials for this book

The materials for this book can be cloned or downloaded from the GitHub book materials repository:

- https://github.com/raywenderlich/mad-materials/tree/editions/1.0

Forums

We've also set up an official forum for the book at https://forums.raywenderlich.com/ c/books/app-design-apprentice. This is a great place to ask questions about the book or to submit any errors you may find.

Content Development

We would like to thank **Rajiv Patel** for his advisory role in overseeing the development of this book's curriculum and sample projects.

Rajiv is designer with over 19 years of working experience. He graduated from the Stanford Design Program, ran a design consultancy company for several years working with startups and companies such as Google, Autodesk, and Dropbox. He was the original designer of the Fitbit mobile app. He is now the design director at Capital One labs.

Image Credit

We would like to credit the following image for its use in Chapter 1, "Book Overview & App Preview."

"iPad Notes App w/software keyboard" by bm.iphone is licensed with CC BY 2.0. To view a copy of this license, visit https://creativecommons.org/licenses/by/2.0/

Found here:

- https://search.creativecommons.org/photos/3101ae9a-6816-486a-b8bb-1736a15b3c13

Section I: App Design Apprentice

Start your journey through designing modern mobile-app UI and UX using fundamental design principles!

Chapter 1: Book Overview & App Preview

By Prateek Prasad

The past decade has seen significant technological innovation. Smartphones, which were considered a luxury not long ago, have become mainstream, and internet connectivity is accessible to a broader demographic. Not only has this enabled users to express themselves in new ways, it's drastically skewed what "computing" means by moving these capabilities out of an office and into the palm of their hands. For many users, a smartphone is their very first computer.

This is nothing short of a paradigm shift that has fundamentally altered numerous aspects of our lives. It's made the world a smaller place by bringing people closer to one other. It has altered our social behavior and caused entirely new industries to spring up. It's mind-blowing to realize that the phones we have on us at all times are exponentially more capable than the computers that landed humans on the moon.

Looking back at how this ecosystem has evolved, we can see that even the entry-level devices available today are significantly more capable than their premium counterparts were in the early days. Smartphones now have more sophisticated interfaces, graphics and animations and ship with many more sensors to accurately analyze the world around us.

This translates into smarter, more capable apps that solve a host of problems — and do it with delight. It's hard to find an industry that apps haven't impacted. It's far easier to reach out to your audience and offer your services if you have an app. This has made distribution more effortless and has leveled the playing field for everyone. But it's also made it more important to know how to design an app that goes beyond pure utility.

Why design matters

With smartphones becoming mainstream, our perception of design and how design impacts us daily has changed as well. With the original iPhone, apps tried to mimic the real world with what's called **skeuomorphic design**. And they did this for a good reason. The iPhone was an entirely new device, the first in its category, so the only mental model users had when they came to it sprang from using real-world objects.

Notes were literal sheets of paper with tears at the top. Contacts looked like a physical address book and there was liberal use of wood and leather across the board. Looking back at it now, it looks dated and maybe even childish to some of you. But it was revolutionary at the time.

As humans, we rely on habits to interact with the physical world. We don't need to learn how to use a notebook every time we buy one because we're already familiar with them. The original iPhone leveraged these tendencies. Coming as close as possible to real-world objects made it easier for users to transfer their habits to a thin sheet of glass and make that cognitive leap.

Ten years later, we no longer need to mimic the real world — but it's invaluable to reflect upon the journey. As technology has advanced, user's expectations from apps have also changed. An app doesn't just need to work. It has to look good, feel intimate and familiar, and be delightful while still being unique enough to attract attention and establish its identity.

That's where this book fits in. It will teach you how to integrate design decisions to your apps. You'll learn how to go beyond merely functional apps to create well-made, well-considered ones.

About this book

The book starts from the beginning, assuming you have no prior experience. It covers all the basics, such as layout and composition, color and typography, flow and transitions, and more. You'll use Figma, a modern design app, to learn the fundamentals of the craft while learning how to use the tool itself. You'll apply the lessons you learn to a sample app for a single point of reference throughout the book.

Movie tracking app

In this book, you'll design **Cinematic**, an app for tracking movies. The app allows users to view trending and top-rated movies and make a list of movies they wish to watch.

Here's how it looks:

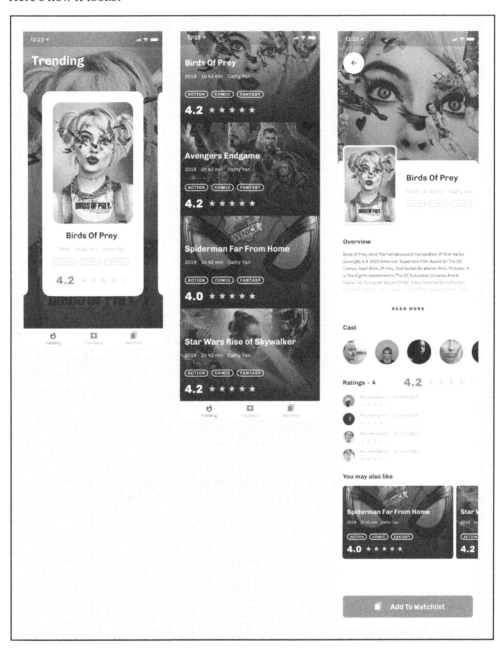

Assumptions about the audience

This book is for you if you are:

- Someone with no prior design experience or training.

- Someone with no familiarity with specialized design tools like Photoshop, Sketch or Figma.

- Unable pay for design tools, unless you can use them as a regular part of your workflow.

- Unable to hire a designer for your projects.

- Someone who wants to do more of the design on your own or level up your skills.

Chapter summaries

Here's a synopsis of each chapter as a preview of what to expect:

1. **Book Overview & App Preview**: This is the chapter you're currently reading. Get an overview of the book including a brief look at what's coming up in each chapter. Set up your Figma design workspace and learn how to access the project files. Jump in and get started right away with a quick project.

2. **Tour of Workspace & Figma Fundamentals**: Get an introduction to key tools in Figma like shapes, frames, sizing, alignment, colors and layers and apply your learnings to design a screen from scratch.

3. **App Teardown**: Trace over provided screenshots for two popular apps to study their layout and identify patterns and structures used to build them.

4. **Wireframing & Screen Layout**: Learn about the importance of wireframing and how to incorporate it into your design process. Create wireframes of a few screens and their components and build a scaffold of the app flow by defining the navigation between screens.

5. **Reusable Elements & Data**: Learn to build reusable components for common UI elements like buttons, toolbars and content cards. Incorporate sample text and image data for more realism. Leverage resuable components for faster iterations and to build more flexible designs.

6. **Typography**: Learn typography basics for communicating hierarchy, order and emphasis.

7. **Colors**: Gain an overview of color basics by learning common practices and creating palettes. Create visual styles for consistency throughout the app.

8. **Transitions & Animations**: Explore the prototyping tools to create a full app walkthrough. Create different transitions between screens to communicate the relationship among elements.

9. **Feedback & Testing**: Explore the collaboration tools to test designs on multiple devices and solicit feedback about the app goals and overall user experience.

10. **Design Systems & Visual Language**: Learn how to build a design system to establish brand consistency. Gain insights into fundamental design decisions by analyzing Apple's Human Interface Guidelines and Google's Material Design.

11. **Recap & Next Steps**: Review of the lessons learned and how to apply them when starting from scratch. Sources for inspiration and useful resources. Suggestions for continued learning and mastering design skills.

Starter files

Each chapter comes with starter files to make it easier for you to focus on the topic lessons, rather than fiddling with setup issues.

The files are Figma files with a **.fig** extension. You'll also have access to final versions of each chapter file for reference.

Setting up Figma

Figma is a relatively new design app that's rapidly gaining popularity. It's comparable to Sketch or Adobe Photoshop, with standard tools for drawing shapes, using fonts, images, colors, etc. It also has built-in prototyping features to simulate interactive walkthroughs.

Some of Figma's best features are that it:

- Is a cross-platform app.

- Is free to use for up to three projects, which is sufficient for this book.

- Has a vibrant third-party plugin ecosystem to enhance your workflow.

- Has apps on iOS and Android, which means you can view and interact with the projects on whichever device you use.

Sign up

Create an account at figma.com.

Launch the app

While Figma comes with native apps for both Mac and Windows, for the purposes of this book, you'll use Figma on the browser to keep things consistent across chapters.

Log in to your newly created Figma account on figma.com

Install the Mirror app

Finally, download the Figma Mirror app for your iOS and Android devices. You can find links at figma.com/downloads or search for **Figma Mirror** in the iOS App Store or the Google Play store.

Taking Figma for a spin

Here's what you'll learn in this first chapter:

- Importing a design to Figma

- Creating a prototype

- Adding a button element to your design

Getting started

Log in to Figma, if you haven't yet. If you're inside a new file that Figma created for you, click the top-left navigation button and select **Back to Files**.

Select the **Drafts** tab, where you'll find three pre-installed projects from Figma. You'll see something similar to this image:

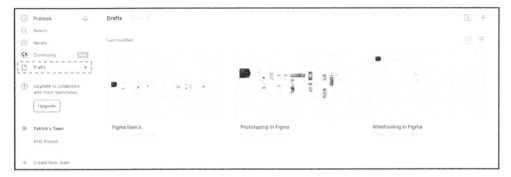

Next, find **chapter-1-starter.fig** in the book downloads and drag it into the Figma app window to import the project.

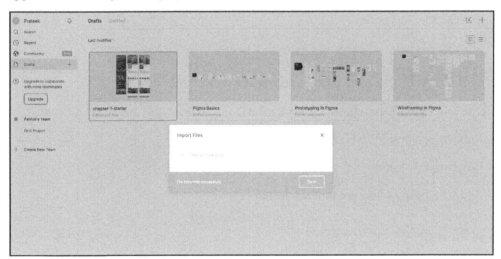

Double-click **chapter-1-starter** to open the project.

The project has three frames that represent three screens of the app. The **movie-list** frame shows a list of movies under the **Trending** category, while two movie details frames show the details of the movies "Birds of Prey" and "Frozen 2".

These screens may look static, but it's an interactive prototype.

Viewing as an interactive prototype

To interact with the prototype, click the **Present** button from the Toolbar. You'll find it at the top-right corner of your screen.

A new browser tab will open with the **movie-list** screen inside an **iPhone 11 Pro Max** device frame. The list is scrollable, but the status bar and the bottom navigation stay anchored.

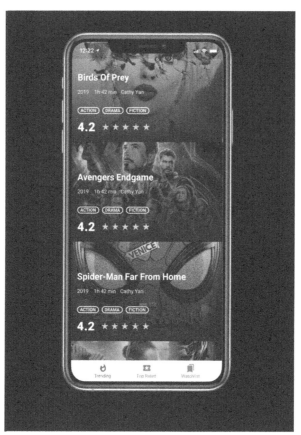

If you click anywhere on this browser tab, the interactive components will flash, indicating where you must click. In this case, it's the **Birds of Prey** movie card, which is the first item on the list.

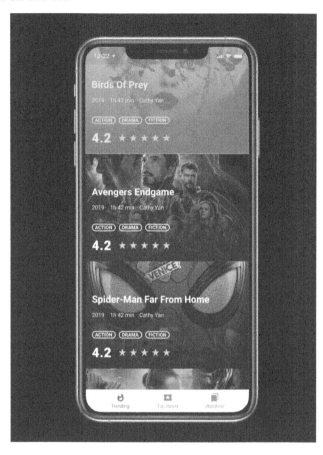

Clicking the card takes you to the details screen for the movie. You can scroll through the screen and see the different sections.

Having the ability to design and prototype the interactions in one tool is powerful and reduces a lot of friction and back and forth in typical design workflows.

As a quick-start exercise, you'll link the **Frozen 2** movie screen to its detail screen. Also, there's no way for you to navigate back to the movie-list screen as of now. You'll build a **Close** button to exit the details screen.

This quick exercise will get your hands dirty and give you a feel for the process. The upcoming chapters will go deeper into individual aspects of the tool and the process but for now, go have some fun!

Creating a link between two screens

Go back to the Figma editor window and click on the **Prototype** option in the Properties panel on the right.

In the Layers panel on the left, expand the **movie-list** frame, and select the **frozen-2** group as shown below.

You'll see a **o** button on the right edge of the card.

When you hover over the **o** it will turn into a **+**. Click on the **+** and drag the arrow to the **movie-details-frozen-2** frame. This links the Frozen 2 card to its details screen.

An **Interaction Details** menu will appear, detailing the animation, navigation and transition properties. Leave everything at their default values and close the menu by clicking the **X** at the top-right.

Click the **Present** button again to view the interactive prototype. You're now able to navigate to the Frozen 2 movie details screen by clicking the card in the list.

Awesome job building your very first interaction! You'll now create a **Close** button to go back to the **movie-list** screen.

Adding a button to the details screen

Go back to the Editor tab and click the **Design** option in the Properties panel on the right.

From the Toolbar on top, click **Shape Tools** and select **Ellipse** (O).

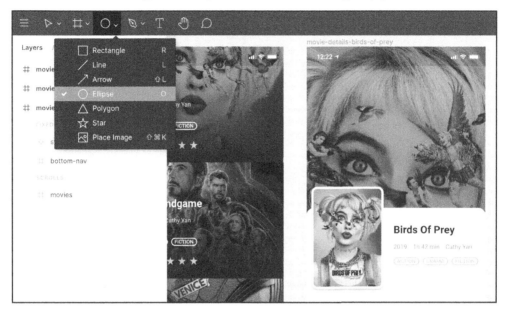

Now, click anywhere on the **movie-details-birds-of-prey** frame. This will add a **100x100** circle to the screen. You'll find this option in the Layers panel to your left, as well.

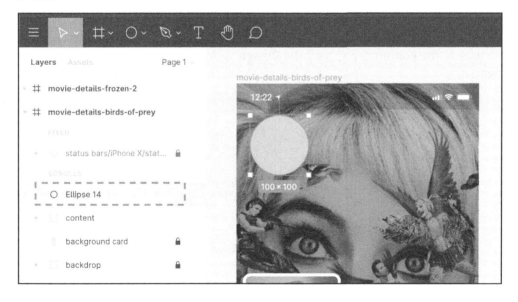

Select the circle by clicking it, then give it the following properties:

- **X** = 16

- **Y** = 60

- **W** = 60

- **H** = 60

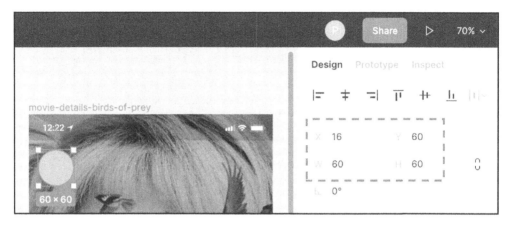

> **Note:** **X** and **Y** values define the **X** and **Y** coordinates of this circle, while **W** and **H** represent its **width** and **height**.

You'll now change the color of the button. To do so, select the **Fill** option from the Properties panel on the right and give it a **white** (**#FFFFFF**) fill.

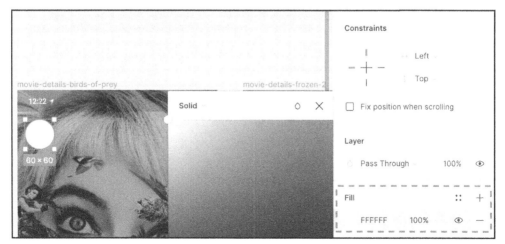

Instead of manually creating the X symbol using lines, you'll cheat a little and use the letter X to keep things simple. Sneaky right?

From the Toolbar at the top, select **Text** (**T**) and click inside the circle to add a text layer.

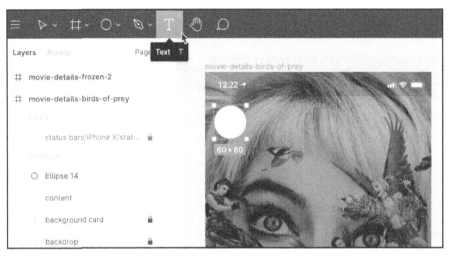

Type **X** in uppercase in the text layer.

From the **Text** section of the Properties panel, give this layer a font size of **32** and use the **Roboto** font with the **Regular** weight.

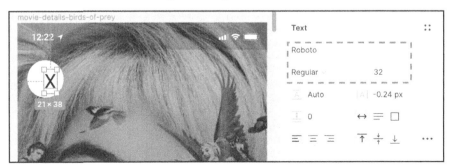

The X is not centered in the circle yet. To fix that, hold **Shift** and select both the circle and the text layer.

Now, select **Align Horizontal Centers** to align the two layers horizontally.

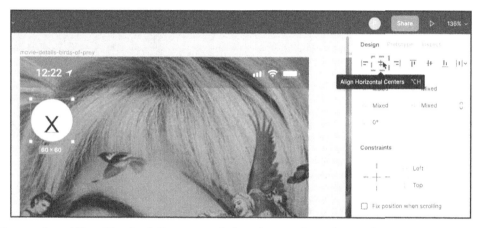

Next, select **Align Vertical Centers** to bring the text into the circle's center.

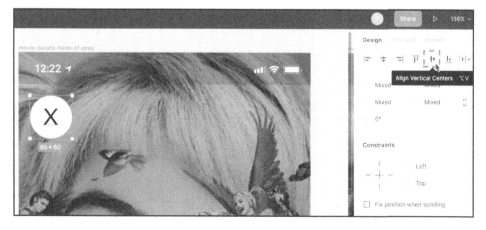

It's time to group the layers. Keeping both the circle and the text layer selected, right-click and select **Group Selection**.

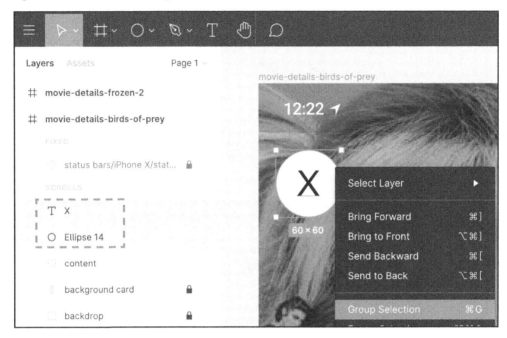

Note: Grouping two layers wraps them into one entity, letting you move and resize all enclosing layers collectively. This comes in handy when working with UI elements that consist of many smaller parts.

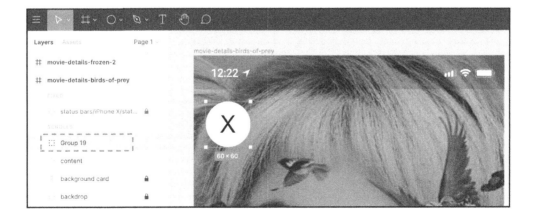

Double-click on the group in the Layers panel and name it **close-button**.

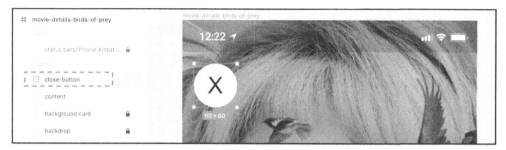

Great job building your first button! Now, it's time to link your button to the movie-list screen so you can go back to the list from the details screen.

Start by clicking the **Prototype** option from the Properties panel. Now, select **close-button** from the Layers panel and click on the ○ and drag a link to the **movie-list** frame.

Go back to the interactive prototype by clicking **Present**. You can now return to the movie-list screen by clicking the **Close** button on the details screen.

You need to add the **Close** button to the **movie-details-frozen-2** screen as well. Instead of creating it from scratch, select **close-button** and press **Command/Control-C** to copy the button.

Now, select the **movie-details-frozen-2** frame and press **Command/Control-V**.

Not only will this copy the button along with the correct positioning, but it will copy the link you created earlier as well.

Go back to the interactive prototype by clicking the **Present** button and you'll see the **Close** button on the Frozen 2 details screen.

Previewing on a device

To take your prototyping to the next level, deploy your prototypes to a physical device and interact with them. Install the **Figma Mirror** app from the App Store or Play Store and log in to your Figma account.

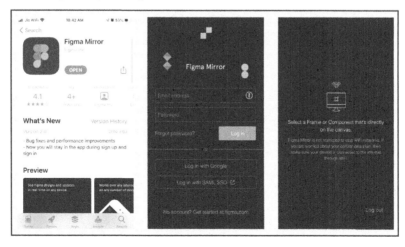

All you need to do now is select the frame you want to view on your device, and voilà, it will appear. It's fully interactive.

Note that the prototype may not fit perfectly on your device due to the size differences, but Figma Mirror still does an excellent job of scaling the designs — close to perfection.

Great job with the quick-start exercise! You built your first UI element and interaction from scratch. This is quite an achievement and you should be proud of yourself. Even though you haven't thoroughly dived into Figma yet, this introduction hopefully gave you a quick look into what you'll finally be able to build from scratch after going through this book.

Key points

- You set up your workspace by creating a Figma account.

- You learned how to import designs into Figma.

- You went through a quick-start exercise to add a **Close** button using shapes, text and alignment.

- You added an interaction to navigate back to the main screen.

- You deployed your interactive prototype to a physical device.

Chapter 2: Workspace Tour & Figma Fundamentals

By Prateek Prasad

In the last chapter, you started by going over the importance of design and how it can help you, as a developer, to collaborate effectively with your design team. You also set up your design workspace in Figma and learned how to import the project files that you'll use going forward. Now, you're ready to be part of the early conversations that steer the direction of your product's development.

While learning how to use Figma is an important part of this book, the most important thing to come away with is an understanding of foundational design principles that you can leverage with any tool.

Tools come and go, and there will always be a newer, fancier one you might want to use. But as long as you approach design from the foundational principles, you'll be able to translate your ideas into real-world designs, regardless of which tool you use. The ultimate goal of this book is to make the tools take a back seat, becoming merely a means to your creative expression.

You might wonder, why pick Figma instead of Sketch, Photoshop or another popular tool? There are a few strong reasons to use Figma:

- It's is free to start with, unlike other programs that require an upfront purchase or subscription.

- Figma plays nicely with other popular tools, like Sketch and Adobe XD, so you can bring files created in those tools over to Figma without issues.

But, by far, the biggest motivation behind using Figma is that it's a browser-based design tool, which makes it universally accessible. As long as you can open websites on your device, you can use Figma, whether you have a Mac, a Windows computer, a Linux machine or even an iPad!

While Figma comes with a fairly minimal interface and toolset, it has powerful features that make rapid prototyping and iteration extremely easy. When designing, you want to explore as many alternatives as possible and iterate over them quickly. You don't want your creative exploration to get bogged down by tedious revisions and adjustments. Learning how to harness Figma's features will help you get more done with less effort.

In this chapter, you'll go over Figma's interface, look at its fundamental features and play with the different tools and options to get a feel for how they work.

Now, it's time for your introduction to Figma.

Exploring the Figma interface

Log in to Figma, if you haven't yet. Then create a new **Draft**. Figma's UI has four distinct sections:

1. **The canvas**: The main area in the middle of the screen, where you'll work.

2. **Layers panel**: Located on the left side, the Layers panel houses all your screens and the components that make them.

3. **Properties panel**: Find this panel on the right side of your screen. You'll use it to tweak and change the attributes — height, width, color, etc. — of the different elements you'll work with.

4. **Toolbar**: This sits on top of the screen as a horizontal strip. You'll find the basic building blocks used to create designs — shapes, texts, frames, etc. — on the toolbar alongside options to navigate your workspace and access Figma's preferences and files.

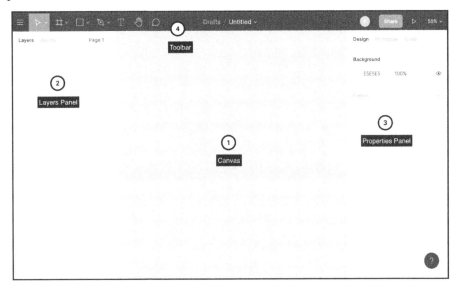

Now that you've gotten a look at the Figma interface, it's time to create the frame where your design will live.

Starting with a frame

Frames are central to any design that you create. You can think of them as containers that house the different elements that make up your design.

Figma ships with frames that mimic the display area of popular devices. For the screens you'll design in this book, you'll use **iPhone 11 Pro Max** as the frame.

Select it by pressing **F** on your keyboard or by clicking **Frame** in the toolbar, then selecting the **iPhone 11 Pro Max** option.

It now shows up in your **Layers** panel on the left.

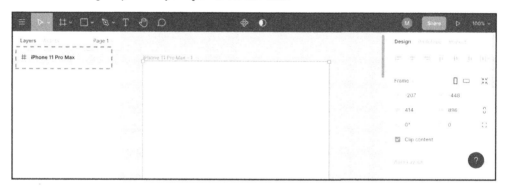

> **Note**: The default frame options are handy, but you can always create a custom frame by pressing **F** and clicking and dragging anywhere on the canvas.

Zoom in and out of the canvas by pressing **Command/Control** and scrolling up or down.

Now that you've added a frame to work with, it's time to learn about another fundamental part of Figma: shapes. In the next section, you'll learn how to work with and style shapes by creating a simple sign-up button.

Adding shapes

Click the **Shape Tools** option on the toolbar to reveal the different kinds of shapes available.

Note: If there's a shortcut available for an option in Figma, it will show up next to the option. In this case, the shortcut to add a rectangle is **R**, for an oval, it's **O**, etc. Over time, the more you use keyboard shortcuts, the more quickly you'll navigate through Figma's options.

Select the **Rectangle** option (**R**) and click anywhere inside the iPhone frame you added earlier to add the rectangle to your frame. You'll eventually turn this rectangle into your sign-up button.

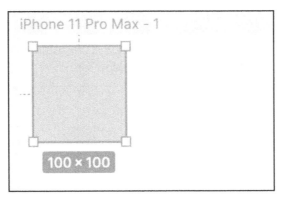

Note: Whenever you add a layer to a frame, you'll also see that layer enclosed inside the frame in the Layers panel on the left.

To modify the rectangle's size, drag the four handles on the corners or edit the height and width in the **Design** tab of the **Properties** panel on the right. Move the rectangle by clicking and dragging it.

Note: When using the handles to manipulate a shape's size, hold **Shift** to maintain the proportions. Holding **Shift** while dragging a shape will allow you to move it in straight lines horizontally or vertically.

Change the size of the rectangle to **252x55** and give it a corner radius of **8**.

X 77   Y 269

W 252   H 55   ↻

∟ 0°   ⌐ 8   ⌐⌐

Click the + icon in the **Fill** section of the Properties panel and select a fill of **#087FA5**. This gives the shape a nice blue color.

Note: A **fill** fills a shape with a specific color. A **stroke** colors the shape's border. The **stroke width** determines the thickness of the border.

For the final touch, click the + icon in the **Effects** section and give your button a drop shadow. Use the default values of the drop shadow for now.

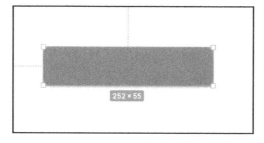

252 × 55

Now, press **T** and click inside the shape to add a text layer to the frame. Type **Sign up**.

In the **Text** section of the Properties panel on the right, change the font to **Rubik**. Use a font-weight of **Medium** and a font size of **18**. In the **Fill** section below, select **#000000** as the fill color.

Your canvas should look like this:

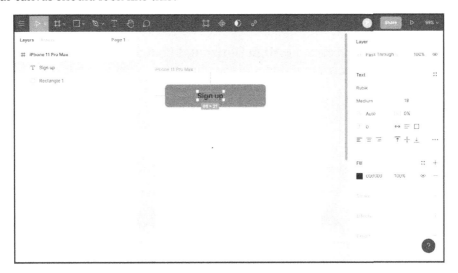

> **Note**: Figma comes with the entire Google Fonts library, you just have to search for the font by name.

Now that you've put the basic elements of a button in place, it's time to learn about alignment.

Aligning layers

The first row in the Properties panel is made up of six alignment options. These options help you align your layers with respect to either your frame or to each other.

Select the text layer and click the **Align Horizontal Centers** option. This will align your text layer to the horizontal center of the frame.

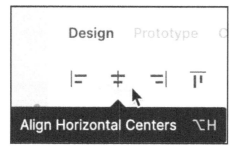

Next, click **Align Vertical Centers** to align the text layer with the vertical center of the frame. Note that this will move the text outside of your shape. Don't worry, you'll fix that in a moment.

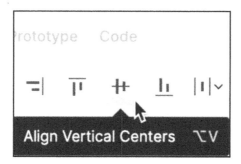

To be sure the vertical positioning is correct, validate it by checking the positioning of the layer. Select the text layer and bring your mouse outside the text layer while still within the frame, then press **Alt/Option**. Red lines will appear on all four sides of the text field, showing the distance from the frame edges on all four sides.

Now, do the same for the rectangle.

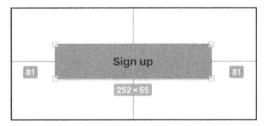

Once both the text layer and rectangle are in the frame's center, you'll group them so you can move them together as one.

Grouping layers

To group the layers, select the text layer, press and hold **Shift**, then click the rectangle. You can see that both layers are selected in the Layers panel on the left.

Once you've selected both layers, right-click and select **Group Selection** or press **Command/Control-G**.

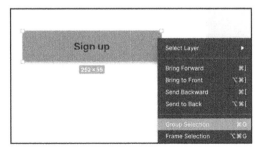

Now, you can move both layers collectively.

> **Note**: You can use the four arrow keys to move shapes and groups around in increments of **1**. This is extremely helpful when you want to align things precisely. To move in increments of **10**, hold down the **Shift** key while you press the arrow keys.

There are four more alignment options, which you should play around with. They let you position your shapes to the left, top, right and bottom with respect to each other or the enclosing frame.

Now that you know a bit about how to add elements to your design, it's time to create a beautiful login screen for your app.

Creating Cinematic's login screen

You'll now leverage your knowledge of shapes, text and properties to create the following screen:

Change the **fill** of the text layer you created earlier to **white** and change the text to **I'm new to Cinematic**. You will notice that the text no longer fits within the rectangle.

You could fix the alignment of the rectangle and the text, but wouldn't it be nicer to have buttons that resize automatically?

This is where one of Figma's most powerful features comes into play: **Auto Layout**.

Auto Layout

Auto Layout lets you create frames that adapt to the size of their contents. This makes it easy to create responsive UI elements.

Press **Command/Control-Z** and change the text back to **Sign up**, then make sure your text and rectangle are horizontally and vertically aligned. Once that's done, select the group and click the + icon under the **Auto Layout** section of the Properties panel to add Auto Layout. You can also use the keyboard shortcut: **Shift-A**.

Visually, nothing's changed — but your button is now an Auto Layout frame that dynamically resizes based on the text.

To test it, change the text to **I'm new to Cinematic** again. You'll see your button grow automatically while respecting the alignment.

You'll use Auto Layout quite extensively in this book. But for now, it's time to set up your login screen's layout.

Creating a grid layout

The login screen's final design has a grid of movie posters in the background with a gradient overlay. There are two posters per row.

Start setting this up by adding a rectangle (**R**) to the frame. Give it a width of **414/2** — half of the width of your frame — and a height of **283**.

Note: Figma supports arithmetic expressions in the fields that accept numeric input. Use this handy feature to create elements with precise dimensions.

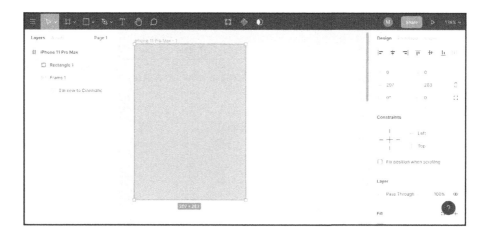

Select this rectangle, then press and hold **Alt/Option** and drag it to the right to create a duplicate.

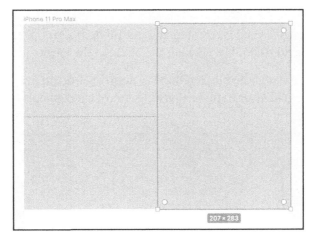

Now, select both of the rectangles and duplicate the row vertically three times so you have eight rectangles in total. Your last two rectangles might go out of the frame, as shown in the screenshot below.

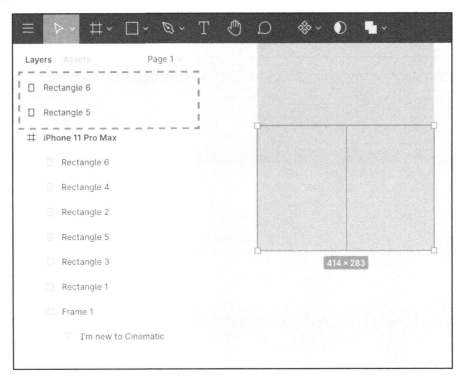

That's because, if a shape's dimension exceeds the frame bounds, it gets added to the canvas but stays outside the frame. To fix this, just select the two rectangles outside of the frame bounds in the Layers panel and drag them back into the frame.

Select all the rectangles you just created and put them in a group. Then rename the group to **posters-grid** by double-clicking the name in the Layers panel.

While you're at it, rename the button frame to **sign-up-button** and move the layer above the **posters-grid** layer to make it visible. Your Layers panel will look like this when you're done:

Now that you have your grid set up, you'll fill it in with gorgeous movie poster images.

Adding images to the background

Press and hold **Command/Control** and click the rectangle on the top left. From the Fill section, click the fill color and from the drop-down menu at the top-left of the pop-up, click **Image**.

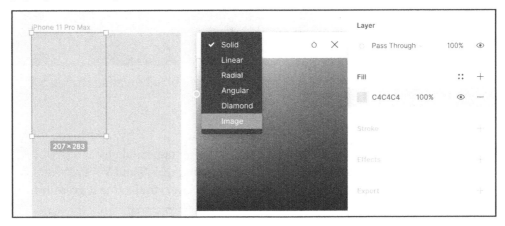

Click the **Choose image** button in the middle of the pop-up and navigate to the **movie-images** folder in your downloaded project files for this chapter.

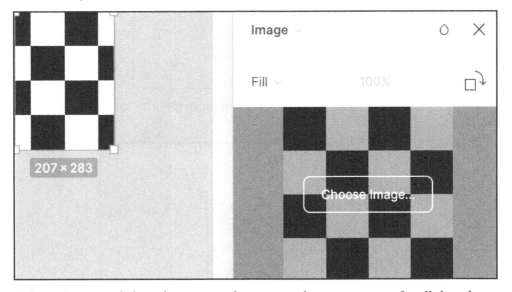

Pick any image and close the pop-up, then repeat the same process for all the other rectangles until you fill the grid with images.

Once done, click the lock icon next to **posters-grid** in the Layers panel. Locking a layer prevents you from accidentally changing it or moving it out of place.

Next, you'll add a background color to make the images blend together seamlessly.

Adding a gradient

To create a gradient background, add a rectangle to the frame and give it a size of **414×896**, which is the size of your frame, then place it at **X = 0** and **Y = 0**. Place this layer between the **sign-up-button** and **posters-grid** layers and name it **gradient**.

Now, from the Fill section's drop-down, click **Linear** to give this layer a linear gradient.

Select the left handle in the gradient slider and give it a color of **#018AA8** and **50%** opacity. Then select the right handle in the gradient slider and give it a color of **#060D31** and **100%** opacity.

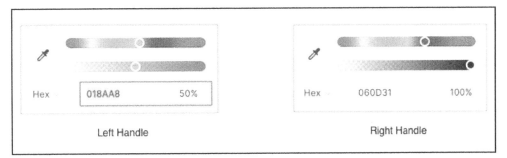

Your gradient layer will look like this:

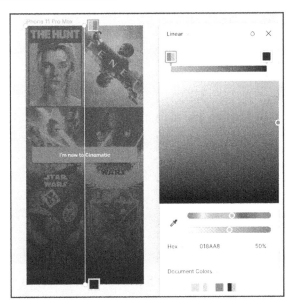

Displaying the Cinematic name

Next, add a text layer above the gradient layer and enter **Cinematic**, the name of the app.

Give this layer a fill color of **white**, a font size of **77**, and use the **Pacifico** font with a **Regular** weight. Add a drop shadow to this layer, using the default values, by clicking the + in the **Effects** section and selecting **Drop Shadow**.

Finally, align it horizontally to the frame and position it **204** from the top by entering **204** in the **Y** field of the Properties panel.

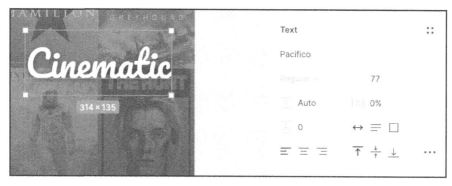

At this point, you have nearly all of the elements you need for your log-in screen. Congratulations!

Adding a sign-in button

The last piece you need on this screen is the sign-in button. You'll add that now.

First, place the **sign-up-button** at a margin of **119** from the bottom.

Now, add another text layer with the text **Sign in**. Give it a font size of **16** and use the **Rubik** font with a font-weight of **Medium**. Give this layer a fill color of **white**.

Align it horizontally and position it **36** below the **sign-up-button** by using the arrow keys.

Remember, you can always see how far one layer is from another by using the **Alt/ Option** button while the layer is selected.

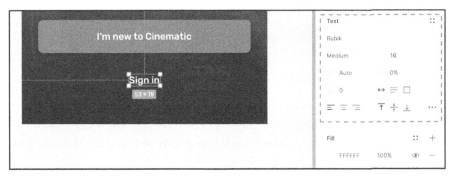

Group the two buttons and rename the group: **buttons-group**. Position this group **64** from the bottom edge of the frame and align it horizontally. Remember to use the **Alt/Option** key to check the positioning.

Congratulations! You now have all the elements of your log-in screen in place. Next, you'll do some polishing to ensure the screen always looks great.

Constraining the layers

Right now, the log-in screen looks great. But what happens if you use a different device than the one you selected for your frame? The design will shift out of place if the screen size is different.

Since you always want the buttons to be on the bottom part of the screen, you can use **constraints** to configure the button group so that no matter what your frame or device size is, the group always aligns itself to the bottom.

Constraints are another powerful feature in Figma. They allow you to configure how your objects and layers are positioned relative to one another, across different frames or screen sizes.

Constraints, along with Auto Layout, are concepts that iOS developers will already be familiar with, but using them in Figma doesn't translate exactly to how they work in code.

Auto Layout and constraints do similar things in both environments, letting you build responsive and adaptive UIs. For Android Developers, Constraint Layout offers constraint and Auto Layout features.

Click the frame and decrease the height to **759**. You'll notice that the buttons get cut off.

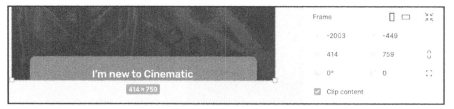

Reset the frame to its original height and select **buttons-group**. From the **Constraints** option in the Properties panel, Select **Left & Right** for the horizontal constraints and **Bottom** for the vertical constraint.

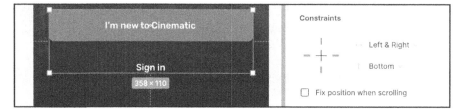

Do the same for the **Cinematic** layer and pin its position to the top of the screen.

Now, modify the frame height and you'll see the button group and Cinematic layers retain their positions, no matter the size of the frame.

And that's it! Reset the frame to its original height of **896**. Your screen in its final state will look like this:

Great job with your first screen! Even though you've only explored a tiny subset of Figma's capabilities, you managed to make a fabulous screen. Pat yourself on the back.

Key points

- You learned about the different parts of Figma's interface and explored the various panels.

- You learned about the concept of frames and looked at the built-in frames within Figma.

- You used the shape tools to create basic shapes and styled them using the shape attributes.

- You learned about the different options to align multiple layers.

- You learned about Auto Layout and how to create adaptive UI elements.

- You explored constraints and learned how to build responsive UI that adapt to frame size changes.

In Chapter 3, "App Teardowns", you'll look at two popular apps and perform a design teardown. You'll break down their discovery screens into their key components and recreate their scaffolds by drawing over them with some basic shapes.

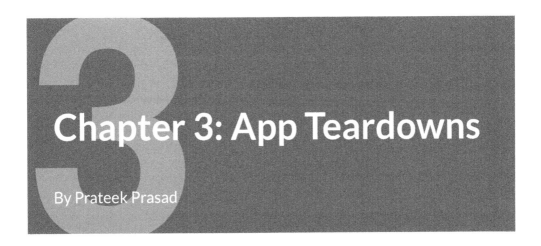

Chapter 3: App Teardowns

By Prateek Prasad

In the last chapter, you explored Figma's workspace and built a sign-in screen using Figma's fundamental shapes.

Before diving deeper into Figma and building more screens, you'll now go through an app teardown exercise to study the discovery screens of two popular apps: Airbnb and Pocket Casts.

Part of developing your style and an eye for good design is drawing inspiration from other apps. Doing teardowns helps you understand why things were built the way they were, while also building your understanding of common layout patterns and design decisions.

Tearing down an entire app is beyond the scope of this chapter. Instead, you'll limit your focus to Airbnb and Pocket Casts' discovery experience.

The primary motivation behind picking these two apps is that their design is consistent across both iOS and Android. This helps you look at the broader picture without delving too much into platform-specific nuances.

Loading the starter file

Start in Figma's Files screen, then drag **chapter-3-starter.fig** into the main Figma window to import it. This file is in your downloaded materials under **Chapter-3/projects/starter**.

Alternatively, click the **Import** button at the top right to navigate to the file and import it.

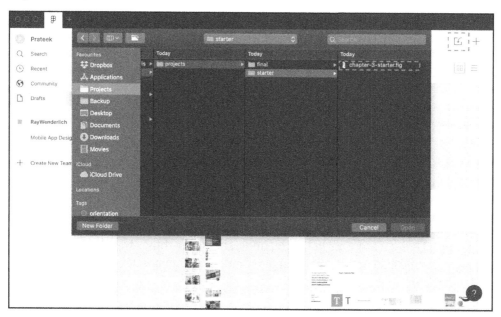

Open the imported project. You'll see two screenshots that you'll trace in this exercise.

While the two apps are drastically different, they're built on the same principles and patterns. Sure, they use different typography, color palettes and layouts to establish their visual identity and brand. But, by looking at each app more closely, you'll notice the repeated patterns and common building blocks that their designers used to build these screens.

Tracing Airbnb's explore screen

First, you'll focus on the Airbnb app. To make it easy to notice the patterns, you'll focus on one section of the app and break it down. In this case, you'll trace the list.

Start with the **Top sellers** section, which has two distinct elements: the section header and the horizontal scrolling list of cards. This section is repeated vertically across the screen for different categories.

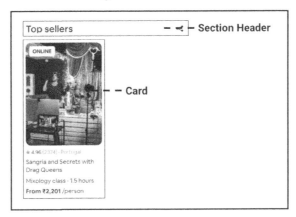

Focus on the card element. It consists of:

- Header image with a status tag and a **Favorite** button

- Ratings

- Name

- Details

- Pricing

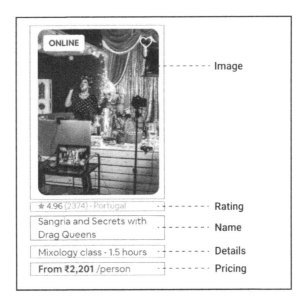

Now that you understand the composition, you can see that the screen is made up of only a few unique elements. What differentiates each instance is the data it represents.

This will become even clearer once you trace out the entire screen. Instead of replicating the app, you'll trace the component boundary to create a low fidelity scaffold. The goal is to gain insights into structure and layout, not to clone the UI.

In the **airbnb-trace** frame, select the screenshot image, reduce its opacity to 10% in the Layer section of the Properties panel, then lock the layer. This will make your trace easier to see.

Select the rectangle tool, then trace over the first section's heading. In the **Fill** section of the **Properties** panel, remove the fill for this rectangle by clicking the - icon and give it a stroke instead so you can see the element boundaries. Give it a corner radius of **8**.

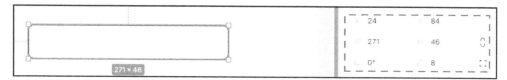

Do the same with the first image card, giving it a corner radius of **16**.

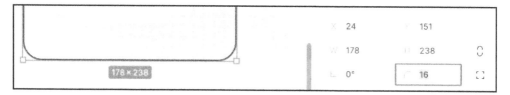

Now, use rectangles to trace the four vertical text sections and give them each a corner radius of 8.

To make this even more effortless, use Auto Layout to maintain the margins while you create the repetitions. You can duplicate a shape by selecting it in the Layers panel and pressing **Command/Control-D**.

When you're done, group (**G**) all the layers that make up the card.

Now that you've created one instance of this trace, you can duplicate the group for other, similar items in the section. Make sure that they're aligned correctly!

Once one section is complete, group (**G**) the list with the section header. Take note of how you're composing smaller elements into larger components that you can reuse.

Repeat the tracing for the remaining three sections of the screen, then hide the screenshot altogether and look at the trace now. Notice how the section header rectangles visually divide the list, even without the data.

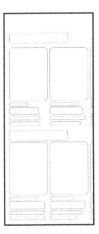

The layout amplifies the screen's core structure, which, aside from the navigation bar on top, is made up of only two components!

Tracing Pocket Casts' discover screen

While the Pocket Casts screenshot doesn't look as straightforward as Airbnb, this method will still work!

Unlike Airbnb, Pocket Casts uses different section styles to surface different things within the same list. The app uses a total of five section styles. Check them out:

Most apps with a scrollable feed of items compose multiple item types to create a list. For this exercise, you'll go top-down and trace the list sections, one by one.

Start by reducing the screenshot's transparency and locking the layer.

For the top section, **Featured**, trace over the thumbnail. Give it a stroke, remove the fill, and change the corner radius to **4**. Do the same for the other text elements in the section, giving them each a corner radius of **8**.

Next, trace the **Trending** section's heading and the **Show All** text, then group (**G**) them into a header. You can reuse this header component across multiple other sections of the screen.

Trace over the list items, group them (**G**) and name the group **list item**. Use Auto Layout to duplicate the trace, adjusting the width of the text layers accordingly.

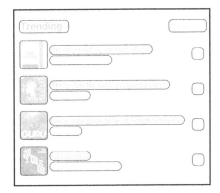

Now, trace race the **Sponsored** section and group it (**G**).

Note: It's a good practice to maintain a top-down visual order in your Layers panel, which means that sections and items that appear first on the screen should be on the top of the Layers list. That makes it easy to find elements when you have to search through many layers and items in each frame.

The **Guest List** section is interesting. Trace the rectangle backdrop, giving it a corner radius of **8**.

Next, trace the avatar image, giving it a stroke width of **4** and placing the stroke outside. Make sure your avatar layer is on top of the backdrop layer.

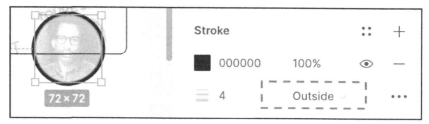

You may notice that, since the shapes have no fill, the backdrop's stroke is visible through the avatar circle. That looks a little out of place.

To fix this, first select the circle and give it a fill. Now, select the circle and the backdrop and click the Boolean operations' drop-down on the toolbar. Finally, click **Subtract Selection**.

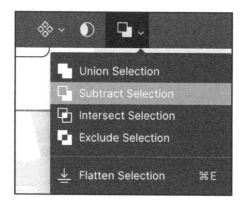

You'll notice that the circle gets punched out of the backdrop.

Boolean operations help you cut one shape out of the other or combine them in different ways. Take a moment to play with them to get a feel of how they work.

Now that you've punched out the avatar, create a new avatar circle on top of the subtracted layer with the same properties you used earlier.

Trace out the text layer and group (**G**) this section. Call this group **guest-list**.

If you've been organizing your groups as suggested earlier, your Layers panel should look like this:

For **The Little Ones** section, follow the same approach as you did with the Airbnb horizontal scrolling list. Trace out the first card and then use Auto Layout to construct the list.

For the **Network Highlight** section, duplicate the **Guest List** section and adjust the trace boundaries.

Finally, for the **Popular in United States** section, duplicate the **Trending** section.

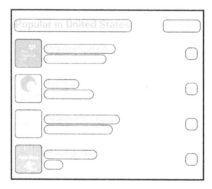

Now, hide the screenshot entirely and analyze the repetition. Unlike Airbnb, Pocket Casts reuses smaller building blocks across components. They also stagger their repetitions.

Great job completing the app teardowns! By leveraging your knowledge of basic shapes, you traced these screenshots and uncovered the fundamental pieces used to build the screens.

A large part of each app's experience was crafted by standing on the shoulders of reusable components with unique data. This exercise lets you see this in practice.

This is a significant realization at this stage, and you'll find that most apps work this way.

As you dive into future chapters, this idea will become more apparent. While you're at it, you'll also learn techniques that will help you fly through Figma.

In the next chapter, you'll start wireframing the screen layout and work on the app flow for the Cinematic app.

Key points

- You learned about the significance of tearing down an app.

- You traced the Airbnb explore screen using the shape tools and uncovered that it's basically built with just two components.

- You then traced Pocket Casts' discover screen using the shape tools and learned about Boolean operations.

- You compared Pocket Casts' trace to Airbnb's trace to uncover how it staggers repetition of components across sections.

Chapter 4: Wireframing & Screen Layout

By Prateek Prasad

In the previous chapter, you went over Figma's basic shape and styling options and used them to create a sign-in screen. You also went through an app teardown exercise to uncover common patterns across two popular apps. In the process, you learned how to reuse and compose simple building blocks to create unique design variations.

Figma has many more tools to offer, which you'll look into eventually. For now, however, you'll leverage the skills you picked up in the last chapter to start laying the foundation for your movie app, Cinematic.

In this chapter, you'll start wireframing the app and build a scaffold that you'll flesh out in the upcoming chapters.

The importance of wireframing

Wireframing is essential in UI design. It allows you to give structure to your ideas and materialize them. Wireframing exposes the rough edges in your thoughts early on so you can iterate them without time-wasting changes and revisions.

Diving directly into creating high-fidelity mockups that look and feel real might seem tempting at this stage, and for good reason. But you are going to start with wireframes as working in low-fidelity helps prevent wasting time and effort.

Wireframing is particularly crucial when working in a cross-functional team because it lets key stakeholders get involved early in the ideation phase to discuss different approaches. It opens up the discussion about which direction to take and promotes collaboration. Your collaborators don't need to know how a specific tool works to provide valuable input.

When you're wireframing an app, it's essential to keep customization and styling to a bare minimum. Wireframes need to be generic enough to allow for rapid iteration and exploration while still having critical building blocks in place to define the foundation of the core experience. This stage in design focuses more on function and less on form.

Establishing the core flow and functional structure with wireframes will allow you to modify and tune the app's cosmetic aspects in the future. In the chapters that follow, you'll build on top of the wireframe, adding the finer details and polish like establishing a palette and a typographic scale.

Defining the app's concept

Before you turn to the drawing board, it's helpful to define the idea you're working toward.

In this case, you're building a movie tracking app that lets users curate a list of movies they want to watch and gives details about the movie, like the cast, genre, duration, ratings and so on.

From the intent above, you can break down the app into a few key features. It should:

- Display a list of movies.

- Show the movie details.

- Let the user bookmark/favorite a movie.

Breaking the broad idea down into smaller features helps you focus on them one at a time without worrying about the big picture.

Now that you have defined these key features, you'll tackle them one by one. As you work, you'll keep the details and finish in the wireframes low-fidelity so you can change things around quickly and create multiple iterations.

Launch Figma and create a new file. Add a new frame to the canvas by pressing **F** and selecting the **iPhone 11 Pro Max** frame. Name the file **cinematic-wireframe** by clicking on an empty spot in the canvas and then clicking on the file name in the toolbar.

Designing the movies list

For the first iteration, you'll create a conventional list, like the ones you've seen in most of the apps you use. The list item will have five components:

• Movie poster

• Movie name

• Metadata (release year, director, etc.)

• Genres

• Rating

Start building this screen by adding a **414×224** rectangle (R) for the movie list item container, then removing the fill and adding a **black** stroke. Align the rectangle to the top and left of the frame by either moving it manually or by setting the **X** and **Y** fields to **0** in the properties panel. Finally, name the frame **container**.

Now, add another rectangle (R) for the movie poster measuring **125×192**. Remove the fill, and add a **black** stroke. Switch to the **Line Shape Tool (L)** and add two diagonal lines. Align the ends of each line to the corners of the rectangle to create an x. Group the rectangle and diagonal lines and name the group **movie-image**.

Position **movie-image** inside the **container** on the left side. Give it a margin of **16** on the left, top, and bottom from the sides of the **container** by moving it manually or by setting the **X** and **Y** fields to **16** in the properties panel. Your list item should look like this:

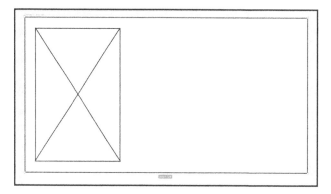

Adding the movie name

For the movie name, add a text layer (T) with **SpiderMan Far From Home**, a font size of **24** and the font **Roboto-Regular**. Name this layer **movie-name**, align it to the left of **movie-image** with a left margin of **32**, a right margin of **32** and a top margin of **16**.

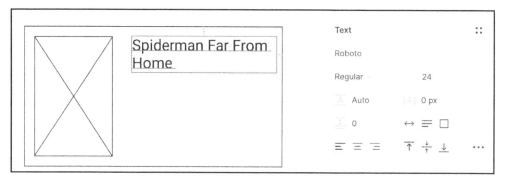

Adding the metadata

For the next row, which contains the movie metadata, add a text layer (T) with **2019** to denote the movie release year. Give it a size of **14** and use the font **Roboto** with a **Regular** weight.

Then, duplicate the release year layer and change the text to **1h 42 min** denoting the movie's duration. Select both these text layers and create an Auto Layout (Shift-A). In the Auto Layout Properties, select **Auto Height** and a horizontal spacing of **12**. Add another text layer (T) in the layout with **Cathy Yan**, denoting the director.

The Auto Layout with the three text layers should look like this:

Name the Auto Layout **movie-info** and place it below **movie-name** with a top margin of **16**.

Adding genres

For the genres row, create a rectangle (R) measuring **51×18** with a default fill. Now, add a text layer (T) on top of the rectangle with the text set to **Action**, a font size of **12** and the font **Roboto-Regular**. Align the text to the rectangle **horizontally** and **vertically**. With both layers selected, change the constraints to **center**.

Next, with both layers selected, create an Auto Layout (Shift-A) and name it **genre**. This makes the background rectangle resize according to the text width.

Duplicate **genre** and change the text to **Drama**. Place the duplicated genre to the right of the **Action** genre with a margin of **8**. Now, select both genre auto layouts and create another Auto Layout (Shift-A) to create a row. Name this auto layout **genres**. Duplicate one of the genre auto layouts and change the text to **Fiction**. Notice that the margin and constraints stay consistent.

Place the **genres** row below the **movie-info** row with a top margin of **16**.

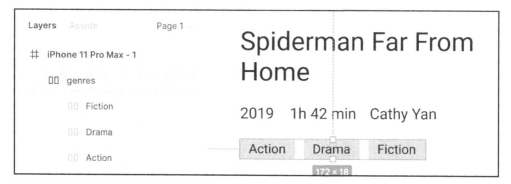

Adding ratings

For the **rating** row, select the **Star** from the Shape Tools menu.

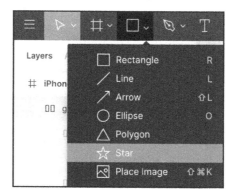

Add a **20×20** Star with a fill color of **black**. Duplicate this layer five times and, with all five star layers selected, use Auto Layout (Shift-A) to create a row of five stars. Select **Horizontal** alignment and add a margin of **8** between each star. Change the fill color of the fifth star to **gray**. Finally, name this auto layout **rating**.

Here's what it should look like:

Place this row below the genres layer with a top margin of **16**.

Group all the layers in your frame and name it **movie-list-item**. Duplicate the movie-list-item four times and, with all four groups selected, use Auto Layout (Shift-A) and name the result **movies-list**. Inside each movie-list item, change the name of the movie accordingly.

This list can be a category of movies like trending, top-rated, etc. In this app, you'll display two types of movies along with a user-curated favorites section. You can reuse the list across the different sections to a great extent, but you'll need a way to navigate.

Creating the navigation

Start by adding a **414×52** rectangle (R) with a default fill and a **black** stroke to the frame. Align it to the bottom of the frame and place it on top of the movies list. This rectangle will serve as a container for the navigation destinations.

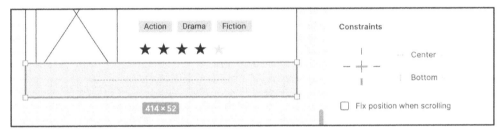

On top of this rectangle, add a **36×36** ellipse (O) with a fill of **#7A7575**. Align the ellipse vertically with the rectangle and place it to the rectangle's left with a margin of **29**.

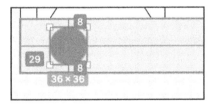

Duplicate the ellipse and align the new ellipse horizontally to the rectangle, placing it in the center. Select the two ellipses and use Auto Layout (Shift-A).

Duplicate the ellipse one more time, giving you three ellipses representing the three destinations. Because the first two ellipses are using Auto Layout the third ellipse should automatically be positioned to the right side of the navigation container.

Group the rectangle and the ellipses and name the group **bottom-navigation**.

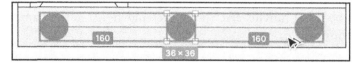

Great job creating your first wireframe! Even though this screen isn't fleshed out with real data, you can see a preliminary structure taking form.

Looking at the wireframe you just created, you'll notice that certain elements will probably stay the same across different variations, for example:

- The movie poster element

- The rating row

- The genres row

You'd make the overall iteration much faster by extracting them so you can reuse them. It's time to take a quick detour and learn about another powerful Figma feature.

Components

Components in Figma are UI elements that you can reuse across multiple design files. They allow you to create consistent designs and make changes quickly.

A great way to visualize this is to consider the rating row in your current wireframe. Imagine you've created ten different wireframes that show the ratings in the form of stars. Each of these iterations has seven movie cards. If you later decide to change the icon from a star to a heart, you'd have to make changes in 70 places! That's a lot of wasted time and unnecessary changes.

This is where components shine. They let you create consistent elements once, then reuse them. When you make changes, you only need to modify them in one place and those changes will reflect across files.

You'll try this out by converting the movie image, genre row, the rating row and the navigation bar into components.

Creating your components

Before creating your components, take a moment to organize things by breaking them up on a different frame. Press **F** and create a new **Macbook** frame, which you'll find under the **Desktop** category in the Frames menu. Name this frame **components**.

> **Note**: You're using a **Macbook** frame just because it is a good size to work in, not because we will be making a wireframe for a Macbook app. You also could have just created a custom frame and set the size to something large enough to provide ample working space.

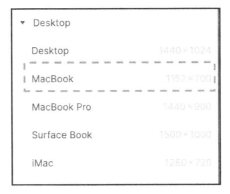

Now, copy one of the **movie-list-item** groups to the **components** frame, then right-click and select **Ungroup**. You can now freely move the individual elements that make up the list item around the canvas.

Duplicate the **movie-image** group, then click on the **Create Component** option from the toolbar on top. Alternatively, you can right-click on the group and click **Create Component**.

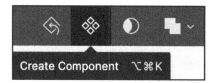

Nothing has changed visually, but if you look at the Layers panel, the movie-image group now has a new icon shaped like four diamonds. This icon denotes that the group is now a component.

Repeat the same process for the genres and rating groups, duplicate them and clean up their placement on the canvas so it's easy to differentiate between individual components on the frame.

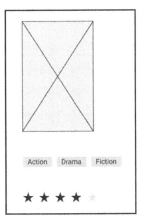

Copy over the **bottom-navigation** group and create a component for it as well.

Implementing your components

Now, in the components canvas, rebuild the **movie-list-item** card by replacing the movie-image, genre, and rating groups with the components you just created.

To reuse a component, duplicate it by holding **Alt/Option** while clicking and dragging it, or click on the **Assets** option in the Layers panel to see a list of all your components, as shown below.

Drag and drop the components you select from the Assets panel into the canvas.

Once you've replaced the movie-image, genres, and rating groups with components, regroup the movie-list-item layers you ungrouped previously. Name this group **movie-list-item** and then turn it into a component. Here's how the component will look in the Layers panel.

Note: An instance of a component has a single diamond icon, while the main component has a four-diamond icon.

Your canvas should now have five reusable components, including the movie-list-item, which is made up of smaller components. Here's what your components frame should look like:

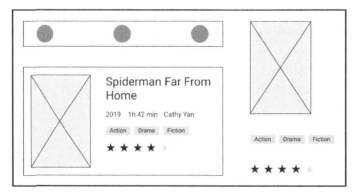

Now, it's time to use the components you just created to clean up the wireframe. In the process, you'll see how powerful they are.

Trying out the components

Create a new **iPhone 11 Pro Max** frame (F) and name it **movie-list-wireframe**. Add a **bottom-navigation** component to this frame by dragging it from the Assets panel then align it to the bottom of the frame. Set the bottom navigation constraints to **Left** and **Bottom**.

Now, add four instances of the **movie-list-item** component to the frame. Change the movies' names, and while selecting all four **movie-list-item** components, use Auto Layout (Shift-A). Name this auto layout **movie-list**.

Time for some magic! On the **components** frame, select the movie-image component and give it a fill of **#DAD7D7**. As soon as you add a fill to the main component, notice that all instances immediately reflect the change.

Now, select the individual genres in the genres component and give them a corner radius of **12**. You will notice that all genre rows now use a rounded rectangle.

Components are a powerful feature that makes iteration and revisions extremely fast. The next chapter goes into components in more depth and uses them far more extensively. If you like what you saw here in this brief introduction, you'll enjoy working with components in the next chapter.

Reviewing the current list implementation

The list looks good, but before proceeding, it's important to spend some time with the wireframe and see how it fits in the grand scheme of things. This is also a good time to refine your ideas and see if your strategy needs any course correction.

You started with the idea of building a movie tracking app that lets users curate a list of movies they want to watch and that gives details about the movie.

You then broke down the idea into the overarching goals of:

• Showing a list of movies.

• Showing details about a movie (synopsis, cast, etc.).

• Adding the ability to bookmark/favorite a movie.

The breakdown was a great starting point, but it leaves many unanswered questions about the app's function.

• Are the movies sorted by release dates or ratings?

• Does the user have an option to modify the list using filters?

• What if the user has already seen a movie? How do we prevent showing the viewed movie again?

• Does the concept of favorites make sense in this app, or should we pivot to calling it **bookmarks**, or **wishlist**?

• Where do the ratings come from?

• Does the year and duration of a movie make sense to show on the card? How does that information influence the user's decision to bookmark a movie?

• Is the information on the list enough for the user and if so, is a detail screen even required?

These questions are difficult to answer because, while some are purely related to design and usability, others require input from the engineering teams and more detailed user research to figure out what might or might not work. Cross-team collaboration is vital to a successful app.

In an actual product development lifecycle, instead of assuming the user's preferences and requirements, you'd involve those users in development via surveys and studies. Doing user research and feedback not only validates your assumptions but also provides valuable insights into how they perceive what you've built and whether it works for them.

It's important to understand that wireframing isn't the only iterative cycle in product development. While wireframing helps you realize the app's core foundation, the final form it takes is heavily influenced by user feedback. This cycle of **iteration ▸ prototyping ▸ feedback** repeats with every new feature addition and redesign.

Prototyping is covered in detail in Chapter 8, "Transitions & Animations" and in Chapter 9, "Feedback & Testing", you learn about how to test your designs and get feedback from stakeholders.

Making some decisions

Since this chapter's scope is focused on wireframing, you'll just go over the questions above and think about the solutions so you can iterate over the design and continue making progress.

• *Are the movies sorted by release dates or rating?*

By default, the list is sorted by release date. This will make sure new releases show up at the top of the list.

• *Does the user have an option to modify the list using filters?*

The initial ideation phase didn't include this feature, but it makes a lot of sense to allow users to filter the list based on their preferences.

• *What if the user has already seen a movie? How do we prevent showing the viewed movie again?*

The user can curate a list of movies they want to watch. This curated list will be a separate section of the app. A bookmarked movie can be marked as seen, which will prevent it from appearing on the main list.

- *Does the concept of favorites make sense in this app or should we pivot to calling it bookmarks or wishlist?*

While the behavior is the same, calling the feature **Add to watchlist** makes more sense. It also provides a clear description of what it does, compared to the other options.

- *Where do the ratings come from?*

The ratings come from an external source, like IMDB or Rotten Tomatoes. This is one of the decisions that the engineering and product teams have more influence over.

- *Does the year and duration of a movie make sense to show on the card? How does that information influence the user's decision to bookmark a movie?*

The release year influences the sorting order, and the duration might be important in certain circumstances. If you have a two-hour flight coming up, you'd plan to watch a movie that fits your flight duration. This is an assumption at this point, but user feedback would help validate and refine the idea.

- *Is the information on the list enough for the user and if so, is a detail screen even required?*

The list shows information at a glance, but a user's decision to watch a movie also depends on many other factors. Some users like seeing the trailer before deciding, while others are picky about the actors. Some even like to spoil it for themselves by reading the plot.

These richer pieces of information are tough to squeeze inside a list, so a detail screen makes sense. The detail screen also gives you space to promote sponsored content tailored to the user's preferences, if the need arises.

Now that you have some actionable answers, revisit the movie list screen. As of now, the only piece missing is an option to filter the list.

Filtering the list

Your next step is to add a button to surface the filter options.

In **movie-list-wireframe**, add an ellipse (O) measuring **55×55** with a default drop shadow and fill.

Place this button on the bottom-right of the frame, above the **bottom-navigation** layer. Give it a margin of **32** from the right and bottom and name the layer **filter-button**.

Constrain the button to the **Right** and **Bottom** so it adapts to frame size changes.

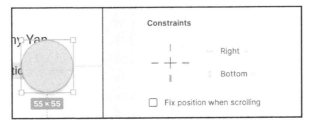

Instead of taking the user to a different screen, it's more convenient to display the filter as a dismissable option in the list screen. The user can filter the list based on genre, release year, duration and director.

Duplicate the **movie-list-wireframe** frame and name it **movie-list-wireframe-filter**. Delete the **filter-button** from this frame.

Lock the movies-list and bottom-navigation layers since you aren't going to make any changes to them.

Now, add a rectangle (R) to this frame measuring **414×896** above both layers. Reduce the opacity of this layer to **70%**, name it **filter-background** and lock the layer.

Here's how your layer arrangement should look at this point:

Add a rectangle measuring **414×448** and give it a white fill. Constrain this layer to the **Center** and **Bottom** and name it **filter-sheet**. This sheet will house the options to filter the list.

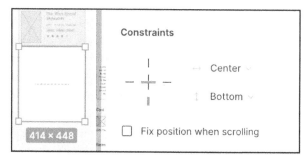

Add a text layer (T) on the filter-sheet layer with the text **Genre**. Use **Roboto-Regular** as the font with size **18**. Place it at a margin of **16** from the **top** and **left** and name the layer **filter-header**.

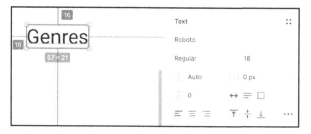

Add a **genres** component and place it below the filter-header at a margin of **16** from the top and left.

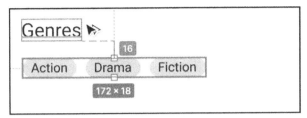

Duplicate the modified **genres** component three times to get a total of 12 genres, as shown below.

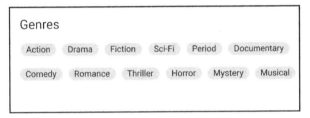

Repeat the process to create the release year, duration and director filter categories. Here's how it should look when you're done.

You did a great job building a good chunk of the filter UI on your own. If you're unsure about the margins and positioning of the different filter categories and their options, you can refer to the final project file, **chapter-3-final.fig**, and see how they look in the finished project.

The list screen now offers the ability to filter the movie per the user's preferences.

Ideally, when wireframing a feature or a screen, you'd build at least three to four alternatives and compare them against each other. This helps you uncover areas that need further polish.

But for now, you'll move on to working on the movie details UI.

Designing the movie detail screen

The detail screen involves a few more bits than the list screen does. This screen will show:

- All the information from the movie-list-item

- The movie synopsis

- Cast details

- Movie ratings

- An "Add to watchlist" option

You'll reuse most of the information from the movie-list-item on this screen. Add an **iPhone 11 Pro Max** frame (F) to the canvas. Name the frame **movie-details-wireframe**

Add a **movie-image** component at a margin of **40** from the top, and change the dimension to **174×262**. Align it horizontally to the frame.

Copy over the **movie-name** and **movie info** text layers from one of the previous frames and change the movie-name text alignment to **Text-Align Center**.

Place the movie-name below the movie-image with a margin of **40** from the top. Be sure to keep everything horizontally centered in the frame.

Place the movie-info layer below the movie name, horizontally centered, at a margin of **32** from the top. Now, add the **genres** and **rating** components to the frame. Place the genres below movie-info and the rating below the genres. Give both a margin of **24**. You'll notice they are quite small for the screen.

Select the genres and press **K** to enter **Scale** mode. Alternatively, you can select **Scale** from the toolbar at the top of the screen.

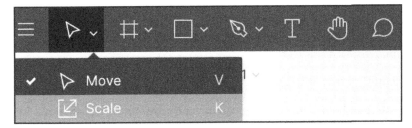

Drag the corner handles of the genre row and increase the dimensions to **218×23** approximately.

Note: Scale may increase your dimensions in decimal values, so you might not get precisely **218×23**. Don't worry about it, as long as you are close enough to this dimension. Remember, this is a mock-up, and things don't need to feel perfect at this stage.

Now, select the rating row and scale the dimension to **237×36**. Make sure all layers added to the frame so far are horizontally aligned.

Next, add a text layer (T) for the synopsis. Don't worry about displaying an actual synopsis here. You can now use placeholder text to get a feel of how things will look with real data in place. A great website to pick up some placeholder text is http://lipsum.com.

Paste nine lines of text onto the text layer. Name this layer **movie-synopsis**.

Center the text and horizontally align the layer to the frame. Use **Roboto-Regular** as the font, with a font size of **12**. Position the synopsis at a margin of **32** from the rating row.

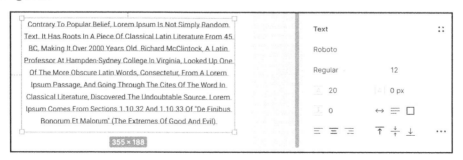

For the cast section, add a text layer (T) for the section header with **Cast**. Name this layer **section-header**.

Use **Roboto-Regular** font with a font size of **24** and place it at a margin of **64** below the synopsis layer and **16** from the left.

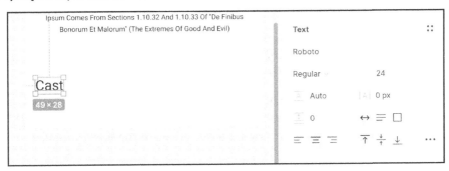

At this point, you might have run out of room to add more layers to the frame. Select the frame name from the Layers panel and either drag its handles vertically to increase the height or manually increase the frame's height to **1587**. This should give you enough room to add the remaining sections to the screen.

Now, add a movie-image component and change the dimension to be **63×63**. Place it below the section header layer at a margin of **24** from the top and **16** from the left. Name this layer **cast-image**.

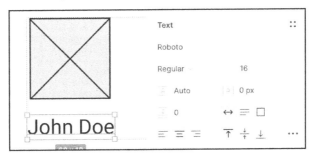

Add a text layer (T) for the cast name below the cast-image with a font size of **16** and align it horizontally with the cast-image. Use **John Doe** as the text. Name this layer **cast-name**. Group cast-image and cast-name and call the group **cast-member**. Duplicate cast-member five times and, with all five selected, use Auto Layout (Shift-A) with a horizontal spacing of **24**.

Now, change the name of each cast-member and name this auto layout **cast-list**.

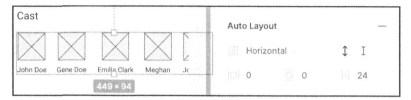

Moving along, duplicate the **section-header** you created earlier. Change the text to **Ratings** and place it below cast-list with a margin of **64**.

To create the rating list, duplicate the **cast-name** and **cast-image** you created earlier. Place the cast-image below the section-header with a margin of **24** from the top and **16** from the left. Vertically align the cast-name to the image and place it at a margin of **24** from the left.

Add a rating component and place it below **cast-name** at a margin of **8** from the top and **24** from the left. Group the cast-name, cast-image and rating and name the group **review-list-item**.

Next, duplicate review-list-item four times and, with all four selected, use Auto Layout (Shift-A). Select **Vertical** from the auto layout properties and set **Spacing Between Items** to **32**.

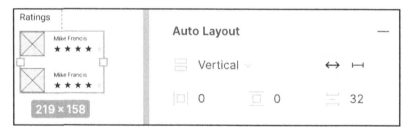

Implementing the "Add to Watchlist" feature

The last missing piece on this screen is an option to add a movie to a watch list. To do this, add a **382×58** rectangle (R) to the screen. Give it a **black** stroke and a fill of **#C4C4C4**.

Now, add the text **Add to Watchlist** on a text layer (T) with a font of **Roboto-Medium** and a font size of **24**. Center the text on the rectangle and group the elements.

Name the group **favorite-button** and place it at the bottom of the screen with a margin of **16** from the sides and bottom.

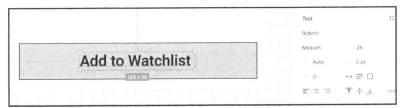

The cast and rating sections are distinguishable at this point, but there's no grouping of the actual movie information. You'll add a backdrop to fix this.

Grouping the movie information

Start by adding a rectangle (R) measuring **379×590** with a corner radius of **8**, a **black** stroke and a fill of **#F5F1F1**. Call this rectangle **backdrop** and make it the last layer on the Layers panel for this frame. Next, horizontally align it to the frame and position it at a margin of **171** from the top.

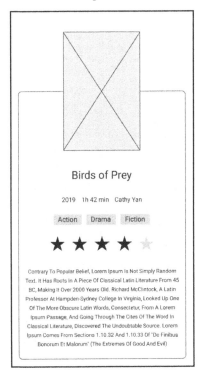

Marking movies as seen

The last thing to do on this screen is to add the ability to mark a movie in the user's watchlist, as seen. This only requires you to add an extra state to the button.

Duplicate the **movie-details-wireframe** and change the button text to **Mark as Seen**. Once done, you should have two states of the detail screen, as shown below.

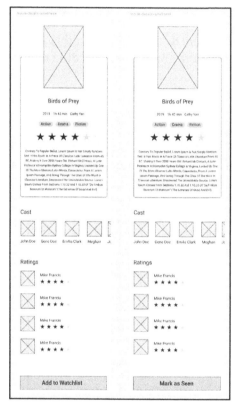

The detail screen looks much better now. The sections of the screen are clearly separated, which lets users quickly scan the information, and it offers controls to curate the user's watch list.

Great job with your first wireframe! You just completed one of the essential steps towards building a great app. By going through the wireframing process, you built out the core of what the app will feel like. Going forward, you have a strong foundation and a clear idea of which use cases you're catering to.

Ideally, wireframing is the stage where developers and designers come together to talk out any engineering constraints that might come up during the final implementation. This gives the designers a clear picture of the boundaries and limitations they should account for.

Try getting involved in the wireframing process next time you work with your designers. They'll appreciate the early feedback and input, as it's much easier to iterate and incorporate changes at this stage, when the designs are still rudimentary.

In the next chapter, you'll build on top of these wireframes and add real data to bring the screens to life.

Key points

In this chapter, you learned:

- The importance of wireframing in the design process.

- How to use basic shapes and minimal styling to build a scaffold of the app.

- Why wireframes need to be low fidelity.

- How to leverage reusability in your designs by using components.

- How to iterate over your wireframes and answer key functional questions.

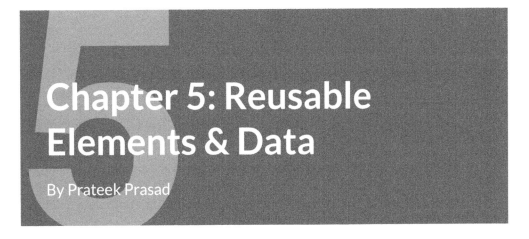

Chapter 5: Reusable Elements & Data

By Prateek Prasad

In the last chapter, you created wireframes for the app and established a well-thought-out scaffold. These are essential steps in designing a product. Having set a general direction for your team, you'll now start working on the finer details by fleshing the screens out with real data.

Among the more useful features in Figma are components, which you briefly touched upon in the last chapter. Even without going into detail, having an overview of components helped speed up the iteration.

In this chapter, you'll take a closer look at components and how you can leverage them to create flexible designs. More importantly, you'll learn the value of reusability when building designs — this chapter focuses specifically on building reusable components. You'll also learn how to better organize your components and their variations.

Visualizing when to use components

A common question when you start using components is: Which pieces of my screen would benefit from being a reusable component? Frankly, it's not a straightforward question to answer.

A lot of this boils down to the idea behind the product and its complexity. The more information your app surfaces, the more elements there are on the screen. But that's not all. If there are variations in how you surface similar information, you'll end up with more unique elements on your screen.

You might have noticed this with the app teardown exercises. Airbnb used just two components to build the entire screen, whereas Pocketcasts used multiple design variations to surface the same information. In both these apps, their underlying information was similar, but how they surfaced it varied.

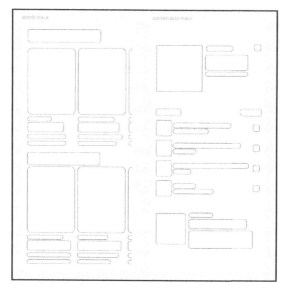

So how do you decide on the component breakdown? A neat trick is to visualize the silhouette of the app. You did this in the teardown exercise. After tracing each screen, you hid the screenshot to view the app structure. Hiding the specific information helped you analyze how many components the screen uses.

Once you've built a wireframe of a screen, it's easier to notice these details. In the future, any time you use an element in more than one place with slight or no variations, you can extract it out as a component.

Getting started

From the project files for this chapter, load **chapter-5-starter.fig** into Figma. You can drag the file into the Figma window to import it.

Open the imported project. The file contains the movie list and movie details wireframes along with the wireframe components.

Building the movie list item

Add a new **Macbook** frame (F) to the file. Name this frame **Posters**.

Add a **movie-list-item** component to this frame by copying the **movie-list-item** component from the **wireframe-components** frame. Select the instance, right-click and select **Detach instance** (Option-Command-B/Alt-Control-B).

Once you detach an instance from the main component, it stops behaving like an instance that can receive style updates from the main component and starts acting like a regular group. You'll also notice the icon is no longer a diamond and the outline goes from purple to blue.

Expand the **movie-list-item** group, select the **movie-image**, **genre** and **rating** instances and detach them from their instance (**Option-Command-B/Alt-Control-B**).

Here's how your Layers panel should look at this point:

Expand the **movie-image** layer and delete the diagonal lines. Select the rectangle and remove the black stroke.

Next, select the **movie-image** frame and give it an **Image** fill.

The downloaded files come with a **movie-images** folder containing posters. Navigate to the folder and select the **birds-of-prey** poster.

To finish, give the movie-image frame a corner radius of **4**.

Customizing the text and fill color

Next, you'll change the movie name to "**Birds of Prey**" and the weight to **bold**.

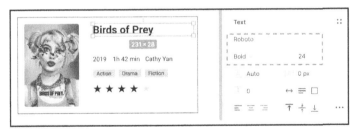

Now, select the individual genre items and give them a corner radius of **12**.

Change the fill of the genre items to **#DBDCB3**.

Next, from the rating group, select the first four stars and change their fill to **#B3C63F**.

Great job! The list item is coming together nicely. For your final touch, select the **container** layer and remove its stroke. Give it a white fill and a drop shadow with **X** and **Y** values of **0**, a **Blur** of **2**, **Spread** of **1**, and **25%** opacity.

Your movie list item should look like this:

The list item you just created looks excellent, but it lacks the wow factor. One of the things that are compelling about movies is how bold and expressive the posters are. These posters subconsciously create an association with the film.

Think about "Toy Story" and tell me you don't picture Woody and the gang. Think about "Up", and the first thing that comes to mind is Mr. Fredricksen and his house, floating away. Imagery is critical in building an association with the brand.

Your goal in the next iteration is to amplify the movie posters.

Iterating on the movie list item

Add a rectangle (**R**) to the **Posters** frame measuring **414x263**. Click the **Fill** option on the Properties panel and select **Image**.

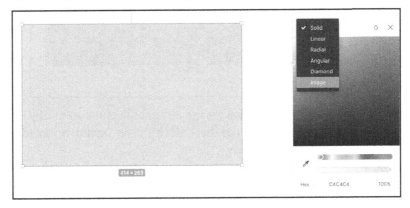

From the **movie-images** folder, pick the **birds-of-prey** poster. Now, click the **Fill** options, select **Crop** to adjust the part of the poster that will be visible in the rectangle and name this layer **movie-image**.

Add another rectangle (R) measuring **414x263** on top of the movie image and align it horizontally and vertically. Give this layer a **Linear Gradient** fill.

Use a black color with an opacity of **8%** for the left handle and a color of **#111111** and an opacity of **100%** for the right handle. Call this layer **backdrop-gradient**. This layer will make the text more readable.

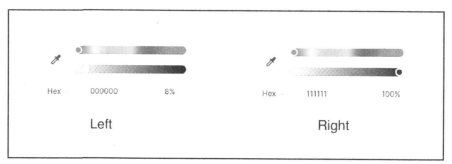

Group the two layers (Command-G/Control-G) and call it **Poster/Birds of Prey**. Duplicate the group six times. You'll need to resize your frame to house all six instances.

Change the movie image for each instance, and follow the **Poster/Movie Name** naming convention. You'll come back to this naming convention shortly.

Make each group a component by selecting the group, right-clicking, and selecting the **Create Component** option (Option-Command-K/Control-Alt-K).

Before moving forward, it's time to do some housekeeping and tidy up your workspace.

Organizing with pages

If you keep creating multiple component frames on the same canvas, your workspace will eventually get cluttered and difficult to navigate. It's good practice to continuously tidy up your workspace and organize it. As the Boy Scouts say, "Leave the campground cleaner than you found it."

To do so, you'll use a handy feature in Figma called pages. Pages allow you to add a layer of hierarchy in your design files by separating things into their own space.

Setting up your pages

On the Layers panel, click **+** to add a new page and call it **Components**.

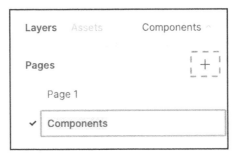

If you can't find the + button, collapse the **Pages** section by clicking the drop-down option, as shown below:

Go back to **Page 1** and rename it **Cinematic App**. Select the **wireframe-components** and the **Posters** frame on this canvas, cut them (Command-X/Control-X) and paste them into the **Components** page (Command-V/Control-V).

Add another page and call it **Wireframes**. Cut the **movie-list-wireframe** and **movie-details-wireframe** from **Cinematic App** and paste them to **Wireframes**.

You now have three different pages to organize your designs and their related components and iterations. Keeping components, wireframes and the actual designs in separate pages makes your working design canvas tidier.

Next, add another **Macbook** frame (**F**) to your Components page and name it **Movie Card**. Add the **Birds of Prey** poster component to this frame. Now, add a text layer (**T**) to this frame with the text **Birds of Prey**. Use the font **Roboto-Bold**, font size of **24**, and text color to **white**. Place it at a margin of **79** from the top and **16** from the left. Name this layer **title**.

Copy the movie-info layer from the **movie-details-wireframe** in the **Wireframe** page and paste it below the title layer. Change the font color of the director, duration and year text to **white**. Place the **movie-info** layer at a margin of **16** from the top and left, aligning its left edge to the title.

Reusing and restyling components

You'll now create the genre component. Instead of making it from scratch, you'll reuse the wireframe's **genres** component and style it.

Create a new frame (F) measuring **250x50**. Name this frame **Genre** and, in the Fill section, change the fill to **gray**.

Now, click the **Assets** section in the Layers panel to view all the available components.

In the newly created **Genre** frame, add the **genres** component. Select the added instance, right-click and chose the **Detach Instance** option (Option-Command-B/Alt-Control-B).

Expand the genres' **Auto Layout** frame and select the three genre groups while holding **Shift** to select them all at once.

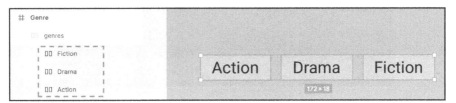

Apply a corner radius of **10**, remove the fill and add a **white stroke** of thickness **2**.

Now, select the three text layers within each genre, give them a **white fill** and a letter spacing of **1**, then change the weight to **bold**. From the Text properties, click the **Type Details** option represented by three dots. Under the **Letter Case** option, select **Upper Case**.

Select the genres' **Auto Layout** frame, right-click and make it a component by selecting the **Create Component** option (Option-Command-K/Control-Alt-K).

Add the newly created genres component to the movie card and place it at a margin of **32** from the bottom and **16** from the left of **movie-info**.

Creating the rating component

Moving along, it's time to build the rating component. Add a new frame (F) to the canvas measuring **250x50**, give it a **black fill** and name it **Rating**.

The black fill makes the rating text visible and helps differentiate between different components in the **Assets** section. Adding separate frames in the canvas for building each component, as you've done so far, also helps consolidate the elements and their related changes into their own section, keeping the Layers panel clean.

Add the rating component you created for the wireframe to this frame and detach it from the instance (Option-Command-B/Alt-Control-B). Change the fill color of the first four stars to **#89E045** and rename the layer to **stars**.

Add a text layer (T) to the frame with the text **4.2** and place it at a margin of 16 from the left. Use the font **Roboto-Black**, with a font size of **32** and a letter spacing of **1**. Align it vertically with the stars, separate them by **18** points horizontally and group the two, calling it **rating**. Finally, make this group a component (Option-Command-K/Alt-Control-K).

Add the newly created rating component to the movie card and place it below the **genres** layer at a margin of **16** from the bottom of genres and **16** from the left. Group the poster, title, movie info, genres and rating and call this group **movie card**.

Now, make the **movie card** group a component (Option-Command-K/Alt-Control-K). You can also select the group, right-click and click the **Create Component** option.

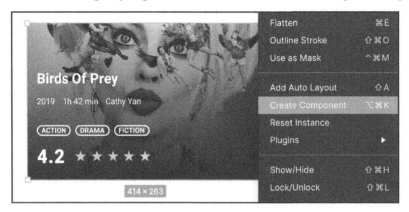

Excellent job with your first fully-fleshed out component! Compared to the original version, it's much more appealing and vibrant. Adding the full-width images gives the design more personality.

Placing the new component in a screen

It's time to now use this component in a screen. Go to the Cinematic App page, add a new **iPhone 11 Pro Max** frame (F) to this page and increase its height to **1578**. Call the frame **movie-list**.

Add a movie card component to the **movie-list** frame. To fill up the list, duplicate the movie card component six times, then with all 6 cards selected, add a vertical Auto Layout (Shift-A).

Make sure the vertical Auto Layout has no padding or spacing, as shown below.

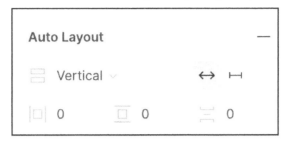

Now, it's time for some fun! All items in the list represent one movie, "Birds of Prey". You want to showcase multiple movies instead of the same one, over and over. To do so, you'll use the instance swapping ability of components.

Expand the second instance of the **movie card** component on the **movie list** frame, and select the **Poster/Birds of Prey** component.

An instance menu will show up on the Properties panel on the right.

Clicking the **Go to Main Component** option, which has four diamonds as its icon, will take you to the canvas that holds this component.

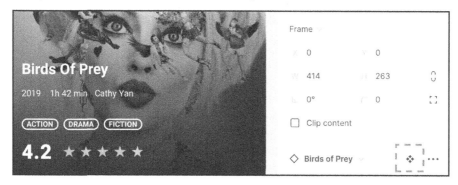

To go back to the instance you were previously working on, just click the handy **Return to instance** option that appears at the bottom of your screen.

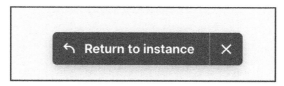

With **Poster/Birds of Prey** selected, click the name of the instance in the Instance section and the **Swap Instance** menu will open with a drop-down of all your components. You can view your components as a list or as a grid. You can even search for components by name.

From the **Swap Instance** menu, under the **Poster** category, select **Avengers Endgame** to swap the poster. Repeat the process of replacing the movie posters for the remaining cards and change the movie names to reflect the posters you use.

Testing the power of components

You may notice an abnormality in all six instances after you rename the movie's title: The title text wraps over to the next line, overlapping with the movie info layer.

There's a simple fix. Select one of the instances and click the **Go to Main Component** option. Select the title layer and increase the width to **350**. Click **Return to Instance** option and your list should now look correct.

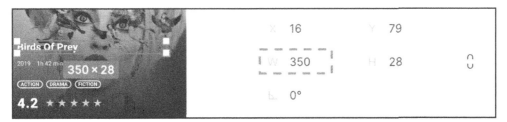

This is the power of components. Suppose this were a list of duplicated groups. To fix the title's width, you'd have to make the change on each card individually. Changing the poster would also be a multi-step process that you'd have to perform six times. By breaking your designs into components, you can make a one-time investment in configuration and reap the benefits across your designs.

Your list looks great. It just needs bottom navigation and a status bar on top. But instead of making them from scratch, you'll see how to use third-party UI kits.

Exploring UI kits & plugins

When designing a product, it's easy to get carried away and want to create everything from scratch. While that's always an option, it's certainly not the most efficient one.

When developing apps, it's helpful to focus on the app's core business logic and use pre-built APIs and libraries for lower-level things like networking, I/O, etc. You could write the entire networking stack yourself, sure. But that has trade-offs, like the impact on the release timeline and maintainability over time. The more abstractions you eliminate and own yourself, the harder it gets to maintain them.

The same applies to design. There are only a few circumstances where it makes sense to build simpler things, like icons, or platform-specific components, like dialogs and status bars. For the vast majority of components, you can and should use a UI kit or plugin. Doing so takes significantly less effort and lets you focus on more essential things like the app's core experience.

Figma has a lot of handy UI kits and plugins to make your life easier. You can find them at **https://figma.com/resources**.

Using a design kit

For the iOS status bar, you'll use a design kit. Open **https://www.figma.com/ resources/assets/facebook-ios11-ui-kit/** in a different tab and click **Open the UI Kit in Figma**. The Figma file will open in a new editor.

Note: Whenever you open a UI Kit in Figma from the Figma resources, the file is copied over to your Figma account. You'll find it in your Drafts section.

Now, look for the **Status Bar (iPhone X)** frame in the Layers panel on the left, copy the **status bars/iPhone X/status bar/dark** component and paste it at the top of the **movie-list**.

Increase the width to **414** and constrain it to the top and horizontal center. Select the **Fix position when scrolling** option to make sure it stays on top when you interact with this screen as a prototype.

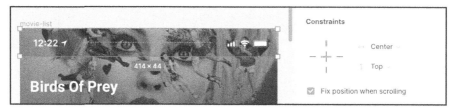

Using an icon set

For the navigation bar, you'll use an icon set.

Open **https://www.figma.com/resources/assets/material-icons-fill/** and click the **Open Icon Set in Figma** button at the bottom.

This file contains all of the icons that are part of the Material Design Icons suite. At the moment, you only need four icons so instead of copying over the entire set, just pick the ones you'll use.

Create a **150×50** frame (F) and call it **Icons**, then:

- From the **Icons — Action** frame, copy the **bookmarks_24px** icon.
- From the **Icons — Image** frame, copy the **remove_red_eye_24px** icon.
- From the **Icons — Maps** frame, copy the **local_activity_24px** icon.
- From the **Icons — Social**, copy the **whatshot_24px** icon.

Paste the icons mentioned above into your **Icons** frame.

Copy the **Icons** frame and paste it into your **components** page. Select each icon and make it a component (Option-Command-K/Control-Alt-K).

Creating the navigation items

Add a new frame (F) measuring **450×90** and name it **Bottom Navigation**. Here, you'll place navigation to bring the user to three different types of movies to browse.

Start by adding a rectangle (R) to this frame measuring **414×56**. Name this layer **background**.

Give it a fill of **white** and a drop shadow with a blur of **2**. Set all other values to zero.

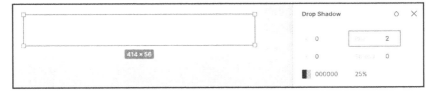

Now, you'll set up the navigation to trending movies. Add the **whatshot_24px** icon. Now, add a text layer (T) with the text **Trending**. Give it a font size of **12** and a weight of **Roboto-Regular**. Place the text below the icon at a margin of **2** from the top and align their horizontal centers.

Select the icon and the text, give each a fill of **#0045D0**, group them (Command-G/Control-G) and call the group **icon**. Add a new rectangle (R) measuring **120×56** and name it **item-bounds**. Align it horizontally and vertically with the icon, group it again (Command-G/Control-G) and name it **trending**. Place the trending group at a margin of **25** from the left.

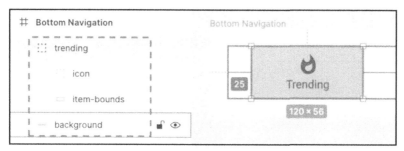

Next up are the top-rated movies. Duplicate the trending group and call it **top-rated**. Change the icon to **local_activity_24px** by swapping the icon component as you did in the previous section, then change the text to **Top Rated**. Change the icon and the text color to **#6D6E70** and make sure to fix the alignment after changing the text.

Finally, you'll let the user view their watchlist. Repeat this process one more time, name the group **watchlist**, swap the icon to **bookmarks_24px**, change the text to **Watchlist** and, finally, change the icon and text color to **#6D6E70**.

Implementing the navigation bar

Now that you have the navigation bar looking the way you want, it's time to use it in the movie list.

Group the trending, top-rated and watchlist layers (Command-G/Control-G) and call the group **navigation-items**. Select the **background** layer and the **navigation-items** layer, right-click and select **Frame selection** (**Option-Command-G/Alt-Control-G**), and name it **bottom-nav**.

For your final step, select the three **item-bounds** layers, remove their fill and make the **bottom-nav** frame a component.

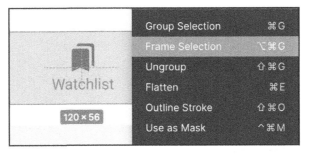

Return to your **movie-list** frame and add the bottom navigation component. Constrain it to the bottom and horizontal center and select the **Fix position when scrolling** option.

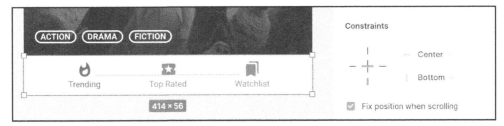

Awesome job with the movie list! It looks really good and the app is starting to come alive. Next, you'll work on giving the movie details screen a similarly impressive look.

Designing the movie details screen

Moving along, it's time to build the movie details screen. Add a new **iPhone 11 Pro Max** frame (F) to the screen and name it **movie-details**. Increase the frame height to **1680**.

Add the **Birds of Prey** movie poster to this layer, then right-click and select **Detach instance** (Option-Command-B/Control-B).

Increase the height of both the **backdrop-gradient** and the **movie-image** layers to **1107**. This distorts the image, so fix the problem by changing the image fill option from **Crop** to **Fill**.

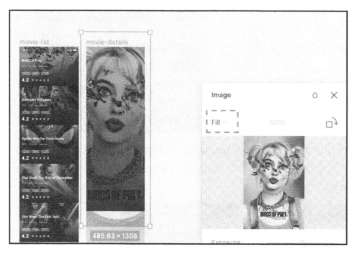

Drag to change the picture's dimensions to **486×1207**. Group the gradient and the picture (**Command-G/Control-G**), name it **backdrop** and lock the layer to prevent accidental changes.

Adding details to the background

Add a rectangle (R) measuring **414×1314** and place it at a margin of **366** from the top. Give it a white fill and call it **background-card**.

Double-click on the **background-card** layer to enter **Vector Edit** mode. You'll see dashed lines on your layer at this point.

Select the top-right and the top-left corners of the rectangle and give them a corner radius of **16**.

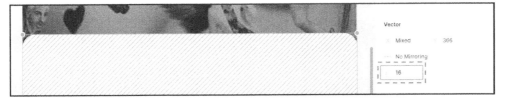

Press the **Escape** key or the **Done** button to exit Vector Edit mode. Give this layer a **default drop shadow** and lock it.

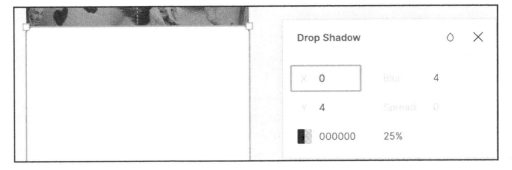

Adding the movie picture

Add a **157×221** rectangle (**R**) with a corner radius of **8**. Place it at a margin of **16** from the left and **323** from the top.

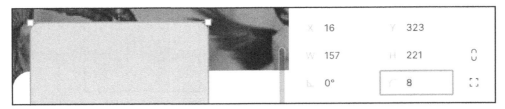

For the fill, select the **Birds of Prey** image from the **movie-images** directory and give it a **default drop shadow**. Add a white stroke of width **5** to this layer and name it **movie-details-image**.

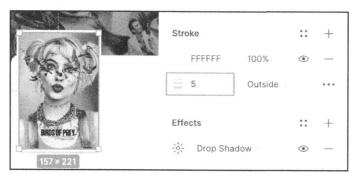

Adding the details

Copy the **title** and **movie info** text layers from the **movie-card** component in the Components page, then place them to the right of the **movie-details-image** with a margin of **28** from the **movie-details-image**.

Change the title fill to **black** and give it a top margin of **36**. Change the **movie-info** fill to **#827F7F** and place it below the title with a margin of **16** at the top.

Add the **genre** component to the frame from the **Assets** section in the Layers panel and place it below the **movie-info** layer. Give it a margin of **16** on the top and **28** on the left from the **movie-details-image**. Select the individual genre and change the stroke from white to **#B9C95A**.

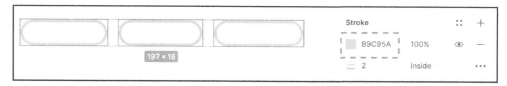

Similarly, select the individual genre texts and change their fill from white to **#B9C95A**.

Group the title, movie-info and genre layers (Command-G/Control-G) and name the group **info**. Here's what it should look like

At this point, you may wonder why the title and movie-info layers are not individual components or why you modified the genre component's colors instead of creating a new component.

Those are great questions, let's address them up before proceeding further.

When to use components

You could have made the movie-info and title layers into components, but that wouldn't have any added benefit. Even if they were components, you'd have to:

- Change their fill color.

- Change their positioning.

For the genre component, you could have created a separate component with the new fill color, but doing so doesn't add value because you'll use that variant in only one place.

Components shine when they're reused. If you're only going to use a variation once or twice, you're better off using an override on an existing component by modifying its attributes.

Setting up the overview

Add a text layer (T) with the text **Overview** to the **movie-details** frame. Use **Roboto-Bold** as the font with a font size of **18**. Place it below **movie-details-image** at a margin of **40** from the top and 16 from the left. Name this layer **overview-header**.

Add another text layer (T) for the movie overview. Place this layer below the **overview-header** at a margin of **16** from the top and left side. Copy the text from **movie-overview.txt** into this layer — you'll find it in the project materials for this chapter. Use **Roboto-Regular** as the font with size **12**. Finally, name this layer **synopsis**.

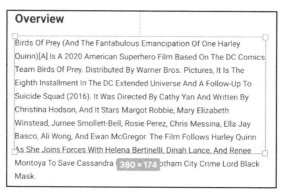

Using masks

The synopsis text is way too long to show in its entirety on this screen. It would save screen space and look cleaner if you show the first paragraph and allow the user to expand to read more.

Another nifty Figma feature, **masks,** will help you do this.

Think of masks as a stencil placed on top of an existing layer. Only the part of the background that's within the stencil's cutout region will be visible. You can achieve a bunch of nifty effects using masks that would otherwise be pretty difficult.

Add a rectangle (R) measuring **380×174**, place it behind the text and name it **background**. The placement is essential to get this right.

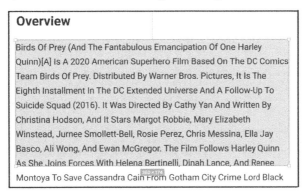

Select both the **synopsis** and **background** layers and click the **Mask** button on the toolbar (Control-Command-M/Control-Alt-M).

Alternatively, you can right-click while the layers are selected and select the **Use as Mask** option.

This will clip the text and the rectangle's icon on the Layers panel will change to a half-moon.

It might not seem that impressive because you could have just copied a single paragraph for the synopsis — but that would make the text static. Now that the mask height influences the text length, you can show as much or as little of the text you want by selecting the background layer and modifying its height.

Fading out the visible text

Now, you'll sprinkle some visual flair over this layer by making the text paler as it approaches the cut-off point.

To do this, add another rectangle (R) measuring **380×174** inside the mask group, right above the synopsis. Name it **gradient** and give this layer a linear gradient.

Instead of dragging the handle across the layer, drag it to the center.

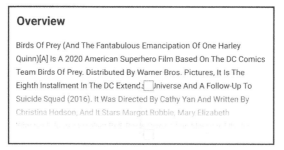

Give the left handle a **white fill** at **0%** opacity and the right handle a **white fill** at **100%** opacity.

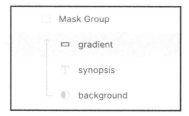

Making the cut-off text readable

For the final piece of the overview section, add a text field (T) and enter **Read More**. Use the font **Roboto-Bold** with a font size of **12** and a letter spacing of **3px**. Under the **Type Details** option, use **Upper Case** for the letter casing.

Move this layer inside the mask group and place it above the gradient. Align it to the bottom of the gradient layer and name the mask group **overview-text**.

Things are looking great! You're finished with the overview section and ready to move on to displaying the cast of the movie.

Adding the cast section

Next up, the cast section. Copy the **overview-header** and change the text to **Cast**. Place it below the **overview-text** group at a margin of **32** from the bottom of the masked layer and **16** from the left. Name it **cast-header**.

For the cast pictures, you'll use a third-party plugin from Unsplash.

Installing and using a third-party plugin

Plugins are critical to a designer's workflow. They help you automate your mundane and repetitive workflows, saving time and letting you concentrate on things that are more fun.

You'll be using the Unsplash plugin to populate the cast section with placeholder actor photos.

Head to **https://www.figma.com/@unsplash** and install the Unsplash plugin.

Once you get an installation confirmation, head back into the editor and, below the cast header, add an ellipse (O) measuring **70×70**. Place it at a margin of **24** from the cast-header and **16** from the left.

Duplicate this circle on the right at a margin of **16**. Select the two circles and create an Auto Layout frame.

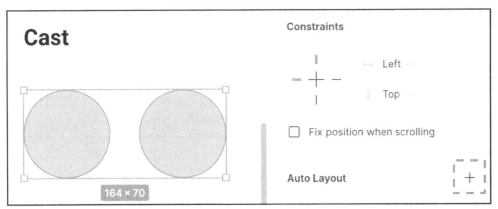

Create a total of **six** instances of the circle in the frame by duplicating them.

Now comes the fun part. Select all the circles in the Auto Layout frame, right-click and go to **Plugins ▸ Unsplash**.

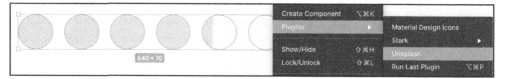

From the pop-up, select **Portrait**. The circles will populate with actual images. Cool!

Adding the user ratings

For the user rating section header, repeat the same process as you used for the **cast-header** and change the text to **Ratings — 4**. Place it below the **cast-images** at a margin of **40** from the top and **16** from the left. Finally, name it **ratings-header**.

Add a rating component below the cast-images section, to the right of the **ratings-header**. Change the dimensions to **208×38** and change the text color to **#727272**. Place it at a margin of **32** from the top and **16** from the right.

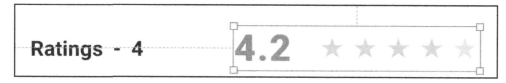

Next, you'll add details about the people who left the ratings. Add a **35×35** ellipse (O) and place it below the **ratings-header** at a margin of **24** from the top and **16** from the left. Name it **user-image**.

Add a text layer (T) to the canvas. Use a name and date of your choice as the text. Use the font **Roboto-Regular** with a size of **12** and a fill of **#727272**. Place it below the **ratings-header** at a margin of **24** from the top and **16** from the left of the user-image. Name it **username**.

Add a **rating** component to the frame. Detach it from its instance (Option-Command-B/Control-B), then delete the text layer with the **4.2** rating value.

Select the **rating** component on the canvas, right-click and select **Ungroup**.

Now, select the **stars** Auto Layout frame, right-click and select **Ungroup**.

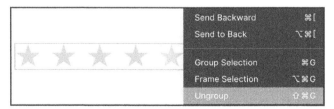

Select the five individual stars in the layer panel, group it back and name the group **stars**.

Change the dimensions of the **stars** group to **86×12**. Place them below the username layer at a margin of **8** from the top and **16** from the user-image.

Change the fill color of the stars to **#F1C644**

Group (Command-G/Control-G) the **user-image**, **username** and **stars** and call the group **ratings-row**.

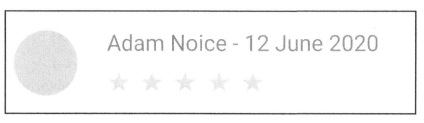

Duplicate it vertically at a spacing of **16** using Auto Layout and then select all the **user-image** layers and use the Unsplash plugin to populate the images. Name the Auto Layout frame **rating-list**.

Adding movie recommendations to the details

For your next task, you'll deviate a little from the mock-up. Wouldn't it be nice to get recommendations for other movies within the movie's details screen? It would go a long way toward increasing user engagement within the app.

Go back to the Components page and, on the Movie Card frame, duplicate the movie card component and detach it from its instance (Option-Command-B/Control-B). Give it a corner radius of **8** and select **Clip content**.

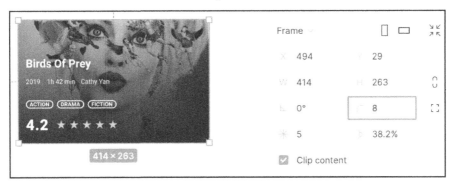

Select the frame, make it a component (Option-Command-K/Control-Alt-K), and rename it **movie card/rounded**. To make it more convenient to swap instances, rename the non-rounded variant to **movie card/sharp**. Resize the Movie Card frame to trim out any unused white space.

Go back to the Cinematic App page and add a section header with the text **You may also like**. Place it at a margin of **32** from the top and **16** from the left. Name it **recommendations-header**.

Below the recommendations-header, add a **movie card/rounded** component. Use the scale option to resize it to approximately **324×205**. Place it at a margin of **16** from the top and left.

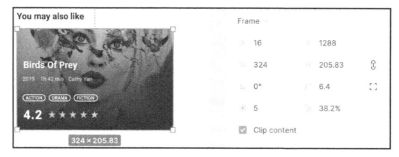

Duplicate it three times horizontally with a spacing of **16**, switch the movie posters as you like and change the movie name. Name the row **recommendations**.

That's a wrap! You've learned about components and how you can leverage them to create flexible designs. More importantly, you learned the value of reusability when building designs!

Why not test your knowledge with the following challenge?

Challenge

All you need to finalize this screen is the **Add to Watchlist** button, a **Back** button and the status bar. Instead of giving you instructions on creating these elements, I'll leave that out as a challenge for you. Here's what they should look like.

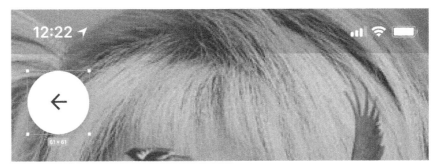

If you get stuck, open **chapter-5-final.fig** and take a look at how it's done there.

Fantastic job building out the movie list and details screens! Your designs are already looking pretty good. While you're still a few steps away from bringing the app to its final form, you should be proud of how far you've come.

The next chapter will focus on even more nuanced details, like using typography and colors to establish a brand identity and consistency for the app. Till then!

Key points

- Organize components and designs using pages.

- Use compose components to build larger design elements and, when it makes sense, to create a component.

- Establishing naming conventions for components helps with instance swapping and logical grouping.

- The Figma community offers third-party icon sets and plugins to make your job easier.

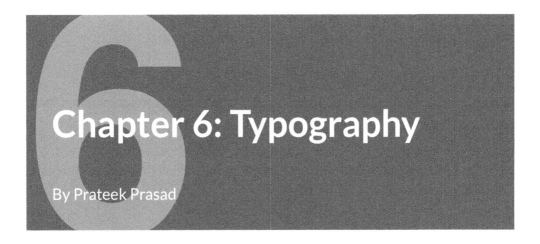

Chapter 6: Typography

By Prateek Prasad

In the previous chapter, you created reusable components that you could use to build your screens. By the end of the chapter, you had a fully functional main screen with a movie list and a details screen with controls to add a movie to a watchlist.

Now, it's time to focus on the more subtle aspects of design: typography and color.

Typography and color are both essential elements of design. It might seem like they're only cosmetic, but they have a broad impact. They not only help you establish brand cohesion and identity, but they also determine how inclusive and accessible your product is.

Though closely related, they deserve individual chapters to drive home the idea and get the basics right.

This chapter will focus on the details of typography and how to build a typographic scale. Chapter 7, "Colors" will go over color theory and how to build a color palette.

These two chapters are my favorite in the book because I get to nerd out about minor details and show you how subtle changes can have a massive influence on the perception and feel of a product. It's one of those things that are rather tricky to get right, but very easy to get wrong.

By the end of this chapter, you'll realize what makes your style choices "good" and how you can leverage typography to add an element of personality to your designs.

While both iOS and Android have established and mature design guidelines for building apps, you won't use them for the typographic scale here. Deriving your design from the guidelines at this stage would be restrictive and wouldn't give you a feel for the process from start to finish.

By building your typographic scale from scratch, you'll get first-hand experience of why things are done the way they are, helping you understand the reasoning behind certain decisions.

Understanding typography

In simple words, typography is the art of arranging letters in a legible, clear way that conveys intent to the reader. Typography affects visual appeal and invokes specific emotions in the reader, leaving a lasting perception about the app.

Emotion? Perception? If you wonder how these are relevant to typography, here's an example: You need to get your wisdom teeth pulled, so you look for dentists in your area on Yelp. You come across this sign:

Dennis Wu Family Dental

This looks familiar and calm, inspiring confidence. If you choose this dentist, you'll probably have a normal procedure and be out in no time.

Now, imagine the sign looks like this, instead:

DENNIS WU FAMILY DENTAL

You'd probably run in the opposite direction from this clinic!

Typography is versatile enough to convey:

AUTHORITY

Grace

When done right, a good typographic scale helps establish hierarchy and uniformity across products. It helps your users immediately recognize your brand.

Before you dive into creating your typographic scale for the app, take a moment to learn some important terminology to help you better understand the explanations that follow.

Mastering typographical jargon

Fonts and typefaces are often confused in typography.

Typefaces are a collection of different type styles that vary in character size and weight. A font is a part of a typeface — that is, it represents one of the variants. In other words, a typeface is a collection of many fonts.

Here's an example:

Typeface	Font
Roboto Condensed Thin *Roboto Condensed Thin Italic* Roboto Condensed Regular *Roboto Condensed Regular Italic* **Roboto Condensed Bold** ***Roboto Condensed Bold Italic***	**Roboto Condensed Bold**

Typefaces are roughly classified into four categories:

- Serif

- Sans-serif (without serif)

- Script

- Decorative

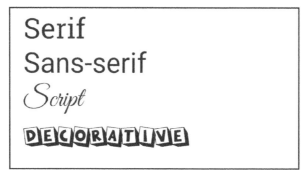

Serif and sans-serif typefaces the most widely used so it's essential to recognize the difference between them. Serif typefaces have a distinguished, extended stem — or feet — in their letters. Their sans-serif counterparts do not.

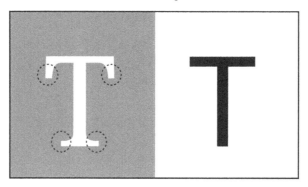

Some popular serif typefaces are: Times New Roman, Garamond, Baskerville and Georgia. Popular sans-serif typefaces include: Helvetica, Arial, Roboto and Open Sans.

Weight

A typeface usually comes in three to four weights. Weight is the relative thickness of a font's stroke. You've been using weights all this time, and now you know what they mean.

For example, the Roboto font comes in six weights: thin, light, regular, medium, bold and black.

Roboto Thin
Roboto Light
Roboto Regular
Roboto Medium
Roboto Bold
Roboto Black

Letter Spacing

Letter spacing, also referred to as tracking, is the space between individual letters.

Upper-case letters have loose tracking, while lower-case letters have tighter tracking.

Design tools like Figma let you modify the letter spacing. This is useful in some instances, such as when you want to create alternate variants in a typographic scale.

Baseline

The baseline is an invisible line that the text sits on, as shown below. Think of it as the lines in a notebook that help you write evenly.

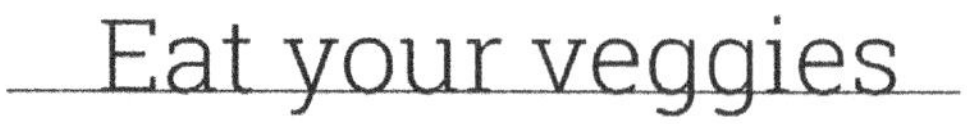

Eat your veggies

Baselines are important to determine an essential aspect of text blocks: line-height.

Line-height

Line-height is the distance between the baseline of two consecutive lines of text. Line-height is crucial for the readability of text. If you use a tight line-height, your lines will hug one another. If the line-height is loose, it will be difficult to break your text into chunks or paragraphs.

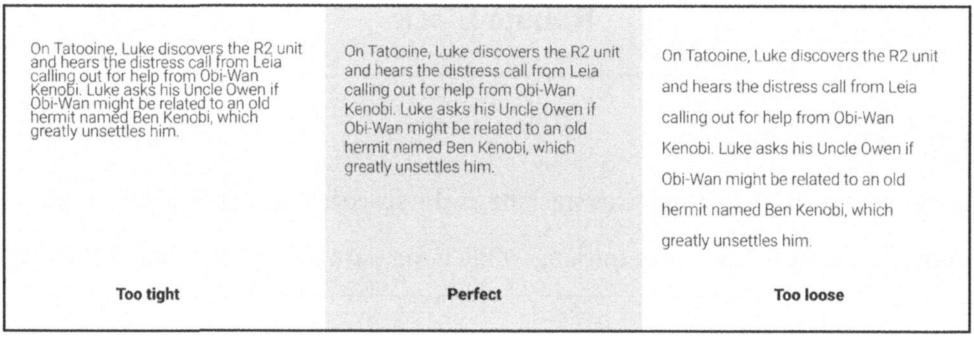

On Tatooine, Luke discovers the R2 unit and hears the distress call from Leia calling out for help from Obi-Wan Kenobi. Luke asks his Uncle Owen if Obi-Wan might be related to an old hermit named Ben Kenobi, which greatly unsettles him.

Too tight

On Tatooine, Luke discovers the R2 unit and hears the distress call from Leia calling out for help from Obi-Wan Kenobi. Luke asks his Uncle Owen if Obi-Wan might be related to an old hermit named Ben Kenobi, which greatly unsettles him.

Perfect

On Tatooine, Luke discovers the R2 unit and hears the distress call from Leia calling out for help from Obi-Wan Kenobi. Luke asks his Uncle Owen if Obi-Wan might be related to an old hermit named Ben Kenobi, which greatly unsettles him.

Too loose

Paragraph spacing

As the name suggests, paragraph spacing is the space between two separate blocks of text. Paragraph spacing is influenced by line-height. It's easy to confuse loose line-height with paragraph spacing, which disrupts continuity when reading.

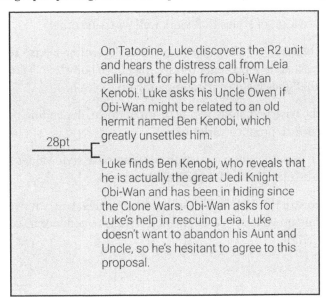

There are many other typographical terms that you won't need for this chapter. If you're curious and want to learn more, a great place to start is with the **Understanding Typography** sub-section of the **Material Design** typography guidelines.

paragraphSpacing: https://material.io/design/typography/understanding-typography.html

Now that you know some critical terminology, it's time to get to work.

Building a typographic scale

A typographic scale is almost like a musical scale. It uses fonts that work harmoniously with each other and complement each other's attributes.

Just as harmonics do, text styles in a typographic scale grow and shrink in a certain pattern to produce a set of styles that work well with one other.

The first step in building a typographic scale is to determine a **base text style** to start from. This text style represents the styling of the body text. Think of the body text as the text that goes inside a paragraph tag on the web.

Once you have the base text style, you scale up or down, depending on your use case, using a **scale factor** to produce variations.

A scale factor is a numeric value. You multiply your base style values by the scale factor to obtain the upscaled and downscaled variants.

You don't have to strictly abide by the scale factor values; you can tweak the scaled variants depending on your use case. The objective is to produce a scale that doesn't compromise legibility.

Getting started

Download this chapter's materials, then open **chapter-6-starter.fig** in Figma. This file picks up where the last chapter left off.

Create a new page in this file and name it **Typography**.

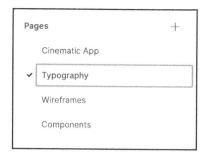

Next, add a MacBook frame (**F**) with a width and height of **500** to the canvas and name it **Text Styles**.

Defining the base text style

You'll start with a base text style with a font size of **14**. Add a text layer (**T**) to the frame with the text **Text Style — 14**. Use **Roboto** as the font with a **Regular** weight and font size of **14**.

You'll choose font sizes for the various elements of your app based on a modular scale, which is popular in web design. Simply put, it's a specific sequence of numbers that relate to one another in a meaningful way. Using a modular scale as a base for a typographic scale makes your text styles scale up and down proportionally.

In this case, you'll use a scale factor of **1.3**, which is a simplified derivative of the perfect fourths scale. You'll start with a weight and then multiply or divide by 1.3 to get larger or smaller sizes.

Here, when you apply the 1.3 scale factor to the base text style, you'll get the following size variants:

TEXT	Hello	Hello	Hello	Hello
FONT SIZE	14	18.2	23.66	30.76

Evening your font sizes

After that multiplication, you end up with types in fractional font sizes — which aren't convenient to work with. Implementing fractional types in code is messy. It's usually best to use type values that are even.

So far, the chapters have all used margins and alignment metrics in multiples of eight, and there's a specific reason why: When aligning and spacing items using increments of eight, your designs scale appropriately on all screen sizes. Most screen sizes today are divisible by eight, which makes aligning things easy.

Naturally, if your type scales use even values, you aren't working with half-pixel values. This ensures a continuous rhythm in your designs, making it easy to manage and to scale things as needed.

This is also a great time to point out that building a type system is not cut and dry; designers often need to tweak values after starting from a base scale. That means you have the freedom to deviate from the scales when it makes sense. Remember, the scale factor gives you a blueprint to build your typographic scale off of, but you should think of the scale as a flexible guideline instead of a hard rule.

With these facts in mind, you'll tweak your values to play well with your designs by rounding the values to the nearest even number. So 18.2 becomes 18, 23.66 becomes 24, and 30.76 becomes 30.

For your next step, duplicate the text layer you created earlier three times vertically and change the text and font size, as shown below. The numeric value for each style represents its font size.

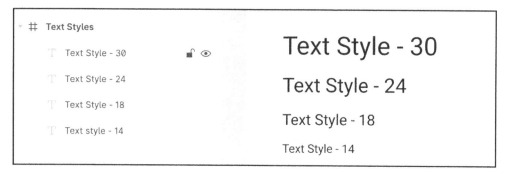

Text styles

Now that you have a basic scale in place, you'll incorporate it into your use case.

In the app, you need text styles for:

- Title text
- Movie info
- Genres

- Rating value

- Details title text

- Synopsis

- Details section header

- User ratings

- Button text

Based on these requirements, your next step is to create the typographic scale from the base text style. You'll work from the top down, with the largest text size first and the smallest ones coming last.

Defining text styles for your elements

The largest text in the entire app is the movie rating, so you'll use the largest text in your scale for that element. To do that, duplicate the **Text Style — 30** layer and change the text to **Rating**.

For the font, use **Rubik One**.

The movie title comes next. Duplicate the **Text Style — 24** layer and place it below the **Rating** layer at a margin of **8** from the top. Change the text to **Title** and the font to **Chivo** with a weight of **Bold**.

For the details screen's section headers, duplicate **Text Style — 18** and place it below the **Title** text. Change the text to **Section Header** and change the font to **Chivo** with a weight of **Bold**.

> **Note**: While the margins and alignment aren't necessary here, you keep the frame clean by left-aligning all text styles and creating a margin of 8 between them. Doing this builds a subconscious habit that will improve your organizational skills.

For the button text, duplicate **Text Style — 18** again and place it below the **Section Header** text. Change the text to **Button Text** and the font to **Rubik** with a weight of **Medium**.

Great progress, keep moving along!

Duplicate the **Text Style — 14** layer and place it below the **Button Text** layer.

Change the text to **Movie Info** and the font to **Chivo** with a weight of **Regular**.

Repeat the same step by duplicating the **Text Style — 14** layer again, changing the text to **Body Text**, and the font to **Chivo** with a weight of **Regular**. Place this layer below the **Movie Info** layer.

Once again, duplicate **Text Style — 14** and change the text to **Navigation Text**. Use **Rubik** with a weight of **Regular** as the font. Place this layer below the **Body Text** layer.

Finally, repeat the same step by duplicating **Text Style — 14** and changing the text to **User Rating Text** and the font to **Rubik** with a weight of **Regular**. Place this layer below the **Navigation Text** layer.

You might wonder why you created the same text style twice for the **Movie Info** and the **Body Text**, then again for the **Navigation Text** and **User Rating**.

First of all, that's a great question and a sign you're noticing the finer details.

You're correct, you could have reused the **Movie Info** style for the body text and the **Navigation Text** style for the user rating text. But having separate text styles for separate use cases, even though their styling is the same, allows you to flexibly change the attributes of one element in the future without affecting other elements. This means you can switch the font of the synopsis text on the detail page without having to worry about messing up the movie info text style.

At this point, the only text element you don't have a style for is the genre text. You could reuse the **Text Style - 14** for this, but the typographic scale would then lack hierarchy. Fonts, weights, and font sizes work together to break the screen into chunks that are easy for your users' eyes to scan.

Supporting the text hierarchy

As of now, the font choices do most of the heavy lifting of creating a hierarchy. So you'll keep that up by introducing a new text style to break the repetition in the scale.

Create a new text layer called **Text Style — 12**, and you guessed it, the font size here will be **12**.

While you're at it, give **Text Style — 30** a font size of **32** and change the text to **Text Style — 32**.

Be sure to change the font size on the **Rating** layer, too. This amplifies the difference between the styles even more.

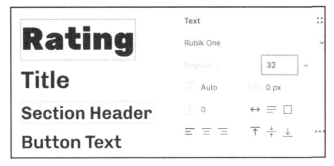

All right! For the final style, duplicate the **Text Style — 12** layer and place it below the **User Rating** layer. Change the text to **Genre Text** and the font to **Chivo** with a weight of **Bold**.

The genres are always uppercase, so select **Uppercase** in the **Letter Case** section from the **Type Details** option.

Now, take a moment for some housekeeping. You no longer need the **Text Style —** **FONT SIZE** layers, so select and delete them from the frame.

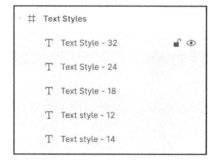

Nice job, your typographic scale looks great. At this point, though, you just have simple text layers and not text styles. You still need to create text styles from these layers.

Creating text styles

Select the **Rating** layer and, under the **Text** section, select the **Style** option. The icon has four dots. Click the + icon to add a new text style.

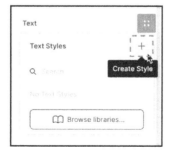

In the pop-up, name the style **Rating** and click **Create style**.

Next, select the **Title** layer by selecting the **Style** option, then clicking the + icon and creating a new style named **Title**.

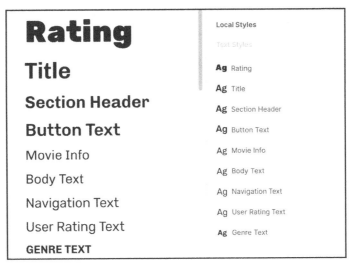

Repeat this process for the other text layers you styled. Once done, you'll notice the styles appear under the **Local Styles** section.

Applying your styles

Now, it's time to apply these styles to the components in the app. Head to the **Components** page.

In **movie card/sharp**, select the **title** layer. Now, from the **Text** section in the Properties panel, click the **Style** icon and select the **Title** style.

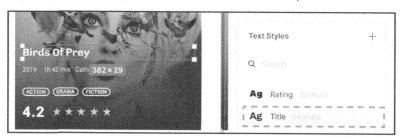

This will update the layer to use the title style you specified earlier.

Next, select the individual text layers in the **movie-info** frame and change their text style to **Movie Info**. Notice that this messes up the **movie-info** section in the design. Don't worry, it's normal to run into alignment and positioning issues when applying text styles.

To fix this, select the **year** layer and increase its width to **36**. That's all you need to do to fix the **movie-info** layer.

Next, switch to the **genre** component, select the individual genre text layers and apply the **Genre Text** style.

Do the same for the **rating** component by selecting the layer with the rating value of **4.2** and applying the **Rating** style to it.

Fixing alignment

When you look at **movie-info ▸ sharp** now, the alignment of the layers is off. Take a moment to fix this before proceeding.

Select the **title**, **movie-info**, **genre** and **rating** layers.

Now, **left align** them.

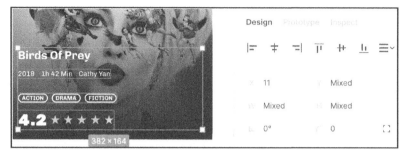

To fix the margin, change the **X** value to **16**.

Your final **movie card ‣ sharp** component will now look like this:

Repeat the steps mentioned above for **movie card ▸ rounded**. If you run into alignment and positioning issues, remember that's normal. If you have trouble fixing them, refer to the **chapter-6-final.fig** file to see how the result should look.

Handling the bottom navigation

Next comes the **bottom-nav** component, where you need to change the styling of the navigation target text. Select the individual text layers and apply the **Navigation Text** style. You'll need to adjust the alignment of the text with the icons after applying the styles.

Improving the details page

Next, head to the **Cinematic App** page. Before you start, check out how the movie list frame looks after applying the text styles. It's really starting to feel like a properly thought-out app.

All right, changing the **movie-details** frame will be quick. First, select the **title** and apply the **Title** style.

Next, apply the **Movie Info** style to the **movie-info** layer.

Now, instead of modifying the section headers one by one, select them at once by holding **Command/Control** and clicking the layers.

For your next step, apply the **Section Header** style.

And... you're finished! See how quick that was?

Finishing your text styling

Next, select the **synopsis** layer and apply the **Body Text** style to it. As you can see, the text is illegible due to the relatively short line-height. You'll modify the text style to fix this.

Select the **body-text** layer and click the **Edit style** button.

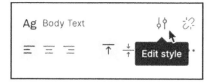

Under properties, specify a **line-height** of **20**. The synopsis looks much better now, and your change didn't affect any other elements. This really demonstrates the advantage of having separate styles for different elements.

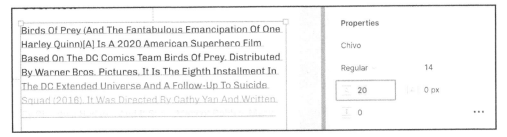

Next, apply the **User Rating Text** style to the **username** within each **rating-row** instance.

Finally, apply the **Button Text** style to the text layer inside **favorite-button** and fix any alignment issues that come up.

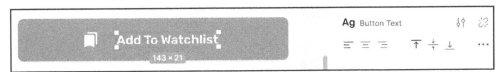

Fantastic job with the text styles! The app finally has some personality, not to mention how visually appealing it looks. This is quite an achievement.

You covered a lot of information here, congratulations. In the next chapter, you'll jump into the world of colors and learn how to build an appealing palette from scratch.

Key points

- You learned the fundamental concepts of typography and their importance in design.

- You created a typographic scale with different fonts and font sizes to establish a visual hierarchy in the app.

- You created text styles using your typographic scale.

- You then applied the text styles to the components and the other parts of your design.

Chapter 7: Colors

By Prateek Prasad

In the last chapter, you focused on learning the fundamentals of one of the more subtle yet influential design aspects, typography. You started with a quick primer on typography fundamentals, then built a typographic scale from scratch.

In this chapter, you'll focus on another essential element: colors.

Note: If you're reading a version of this book printed in grayscale, I've included colored versions of the screenshots from the informational sections of this chapter with the project files. I highly recommend looking at them while reviewing the informational sections.

Colors, like typography, play a vital role in design — as well as in everyday life. Colors evoke certain emotions and elicit a deep psychological response in our brain.

Colors convey information without words.

When you use them correctly and tastefully, colors help users and provide visual feedback for eventful interactions, like highlighting errors and providing confirmation.

Colors are crucial for establishing brand identity and helping a product stand out. They bring uniformity and cohesion to a family of related products. While they're a subtle aspect of design, colors make a big impact on how users perceive and remember your brand.

Great examples of products that leverage color to establish their identity are Coca-Cola's brilliant red, McLaren's papaya orange and Apple's use of white across their products and packaging. Often underrated, colors build an instant association with a brand identity.

Before getting into building a palette, you'll walk through some fundamental concepts of color theory to help you pick the right colors for your project.

Basics of color theory

Simply put, color theory is a collection of guidelines that designers use to pick colors. These guidelines are based upon how humans perceive colors, which emotions and messages they convey and what visual effects you can achieve when you mix them.

Now, you'll start from the ground up by understanding what a color is.

Color is a perception. When our eyes see an object, they send signals to our brains, which our brains use to define the color.

These signals are wavelengths of light reflected by objects.

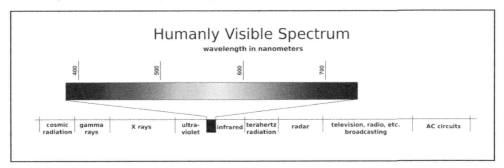

Color wheel

The first color wheel was designed by Sir Isaac Newton in the 1600s. Designers still use it today to mix and match colors to build a palette.

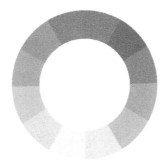

A color wheel contains:

Three primary colors:

- Red

- Yellow

- Blue

Three secondary colors, derived from mixing the primary colors:

- Blue plus yellow = green

- Red plus yellow = orange

- Blue plus red = purple

Six tertiary colors, derived from mixing the primary and secondary colors:

- Red-orange

- Red-purple

- Blue-purple

- Blue-green

- Yellow-green

- Yellow-orange

Hue

Hue is the name of the color: red, blue, green, yellow, orange and so on.

Saturation

Saturation is the intensity or purity of a hue. High saturation makes a color look bright and vibrant, whereas a desaturated color is more washed out and subtle.

Value

Value determines the degree of darkness or lightness of a hue, ranging from pure white to pure black.

Shade

A shade is a hue produced by adding black in varying amounts. The image below shows various shades of red with increasing amounts of black added to it.

Tint

A tint is a hue produced by adding white in varying amounts. The image below shows various tints of red with increasing amounts of white added to it.

Color Temperature

Divide the color wheel vertically into two halves. The colors on the left half are the **warm** colors — reds, oranges and yellows. The ones on the right half are the **cool** colors — purples, blues and greens.

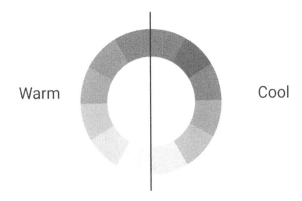

Warm   Cool

Contrast

In color theory, contrast is the difference in the visual properties of an object that distinguishes it from other objects and its own background.

In other words, it's the difference between two colors.

In web and mobile design, using contrasting colors is essential to ensuring accessibility and readability. You must always strive to create designs that have a strong contrast between the content and background to ensure users with visual impairments aren't left out.

The **Web Content Accessibility Guidelines (WCAG) 2** recommends a minimum contrast ratio of

- **4.5:1** for regular text.

- **3:1** for large text, graphics and user interface components.

There are several online tools available to check the contrast ratios of your colors, like WebAIM's contrast checker: webaim.org/resources/contrastchecker/.

You can feed the background and foreground colors into this tool and get the resulting ratio. These ratios are measured using a grading system called **levels of conformance**. The highest achievable grade on this system is **AAA**, which requires a **7:1** ratio.

In the image below, you can see an example of a poor contrast ratio:

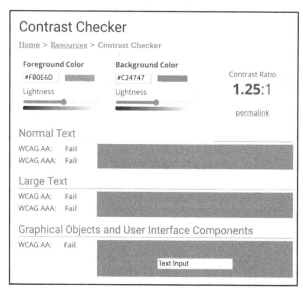

In comparison, here's what a good contrast ratio looks like:

Sometimes, you can't — or shouldn't try to — achieve the **AAA** grade, as it requires highly complementary colors, which might make your palette dull or unappealing.

Now that you have a basic understanding of colors and contrast, it's time to understand how to pick colors using tried and tested color schemes.

Color schemes

Color schemes are formulas based on color harmony. In color theory, color harmonies are sets of colors that look good together.

Monochromatic scheme

The simplest form of a color scheme is the monochromatic color scheme. You start with a single color on the color wheel, then create variations using the knowledge of saturation and values.

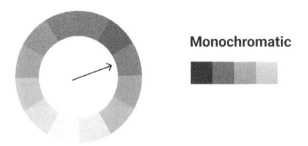

Analogous scheme

An analogous color scheme uses colors next to each other on the color wheel, like reds and oranges or greens and blues.

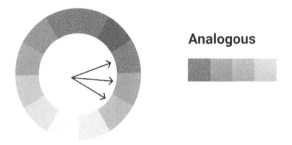

Complementary scheme

A complementary color scheme uses colors opposite one other on the color wheel, like blue and orange or red and green.

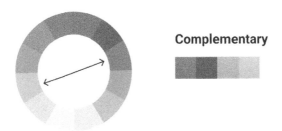

Split complementary scheme

A split complementary color scheme uses colors on either side of the complement of the base color. This scheme provides the same contrast level as the complementary scheme, but gives you more colors to work with.

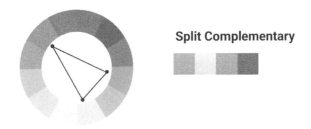

Triadic scheme

A triadic color scheme uses three colors that are evenly spaced on the color wheel, forming a perfect triangle.

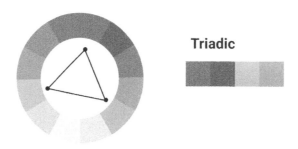

Tetradic scheme

A tetradic color scheme uses four colors that form a rectangle on the color wheel, and the diagonals are complementary pairs.

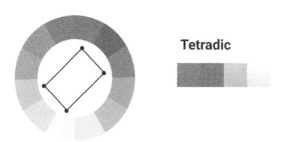

It's worth noting that color schemes are guidelines, or a starting point to build your palette. They aren't hard rules you must follow. Depending on your use case, your brand needs and your contrast constraints, feel free to tweak properties as and when you need to.

Whichever color scheme you choose, it's important that the palette you choose doesn't hamper the legibility and readability of text on your product.

Finding the right scheme for your project

While colors are an important part of design, they're by no means a must-have requirement for every project, whether print or digital. An informational website, like a blog or an online journal, can deliver a great experience while sticking to a monochromatic palette that uses black text on a white background.

The app you're working on doesn't use colors heavily because it relies on the movie posters for vibrancy. That said, the app still uses colors for visual feedback, like the states of the bottom navigation buttons, the ratings component and the **Add to Watchlist** button.

Generating and experimenting with different palettes is outside the scope of this chapter, as you often need to account for the brand guidelines of the company. Still, if you want to generate and test different color combinations for your projects, check out the following:

- **Adobe Colors**: https://color.adobe.com

- **Material Color Tool**: https://material.io/resources/color

With these resources, you can use what you've learned here to quickly build and experiment with different color styles.

You've only scratched the surface of color theory here, but you've learned enough to get started.

Building your palette

Compared to building the type scale, your palette is much more straightforward because you'll just convert the colors you're already using into reusable styles. This saves you the trouble of manually copy-pasting the hex codes going forward.

At this point, you might wonder what the idea behind selecting Cinematic's colors was.

The movie posters in the app are already vibrant and loud enough to draw the user's attention. Any additional colors you use for UI elements, like buttons and ratings, must be bold and vibrant enough to make it easy for users to discover these interactions and not feel lost.

That was the primary motivation behind picking the current palette. The palette uses the triadic color scheme with the saturation of each color cranked up to eleven!

Now that you know the reasoning behind selecting the palette, it's time to build the color styles.

Download this chapter's materials, then open **chapter-7-starter.fig** in Figma. This file picks up where the last chapter left off.

Turning your colors into reusable styles

Now, it's time to finalize the color styles for this app. Create a new page and name it **Colors**.

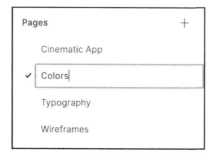

Add a new **400×300** frame (**F**) to the canvas.

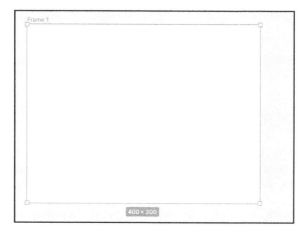

Name this frame **Palette**. Add a **30×30** ellipse (**O**) to the frame and give it a fill of **#F34444**.

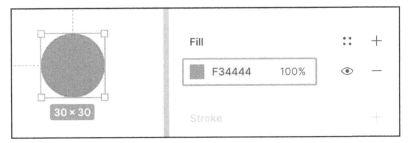

Creating a color style is relatively straightforward. In the **Fill** section, click on the **Style** icon, which looks like four circles.

In the menu that pops up, click the **+** icon and name this style **button/primary**.

The **category/subcategory** notation lets you create categories within the styles.

Add another **30×30** ellipse (**O**) and give it a fill of **#6D6E70**. Then create a new style and name it **navigation/inactive**.

The active icon in the navigation has a deep blue color, so create a new **30×30** ellipse (**O**) for it and give it a fill of **#0045D0**. Finally, create a new style named **navigation/ active**.

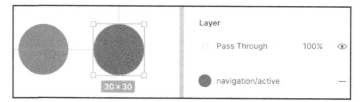

Why aren't you focusing on the circles' position and alignment? That's because, once you create a color style, you can delete the circle and the style is still available for you to use.

You want to quickly build a palette so you can apply the styles to your designs. Nevertheless, you should keep a rudimentary arrangement in place so it's easy to differentiate between different styles.

Creating the text color styles

Keep moving along to create the text color styles. Add another **30×30** ellipse (**O**) and give it a **#000000** fill and create a style named **text/primary**.

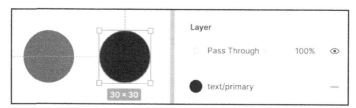

Create another **30×30** ellipse (**O**) with a **#ffffff** fill. At this point, the white circle isn't visible because the frame you're working on is also white.

To create contrast between the frame and the individual color styles, change the frame's fill color to **#D2D2D2**. This will differentiate between the styles and the frame.

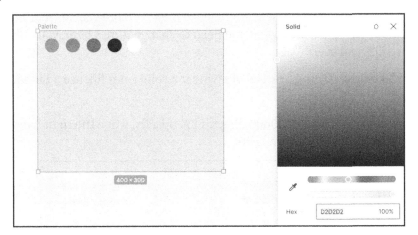

Create a new color style from the circle with white fill and name it **text/secondary**.

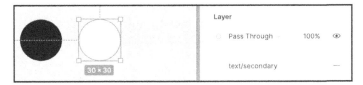

Create another **30×30** ellipse (**O**) with a fill of **#B9C95A** and name this color **text/accent**.

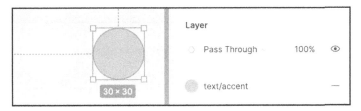

Finally, create still another **30×30** ellipse (**O**) with a fill of **#727272** and name this color **text/muted**.

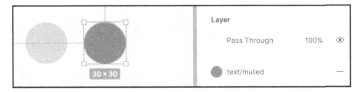

Using gradients in color styles

Color styles aren't limited to solid fills; they can also hold gradients. The movie posters in the app use a gradient scrim to make the text more visible. Your next step is to make this gradient a style, so if you need to change things later, you only need to do it in a single place.

Add a **30×30** ellipse (**O**) and, instead of giving it a solid color fill, use a **Linear** gradient.

The left handle will have a **#000000** fill with **8%** opacity, while the right handle will have a **#000000** fill with **100%** opacity.

Create a new style using this circle and name it **gradient/poster**.

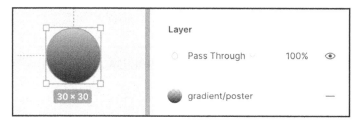

Styling the rating component

For your final step in defining your palette, you'll create styles for your rating component.

Add a **30×30** ellipse (**O**) with a fill of **#89E045** and name it **rating/positive**.

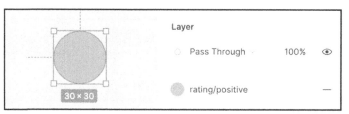

Create another ellipse (**O**) and give it a fill of **#C4C4C4**, which also happens to be the default fill color in Figma. Name this style **rating/neutral**.

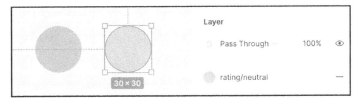

And that's it! Great job building your color style catalog. If you deselect everything on the canvas, you'll see all your color styles appear on the right.

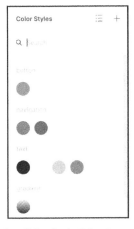

The naming schematic you used will be helpful when assigning styles to your components.

Applying the color styles

Head to your **Components** page to apply the color styles you just created. First up: the posters. Select the **backdrop-gradient** layer from the **Poster/Birds of Prey** component.

Now, click the **Fill** section's **Style** button.

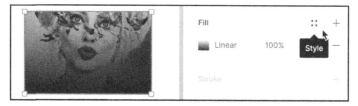

Select the **gradient/poster** style to remove the existing fill and apply the color style.

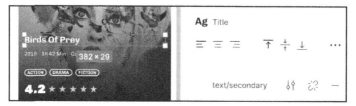

Repeat this process for the remaining posters.

> **Note**: Instead of manually applying the styles one by one, press and hold **Command/Control-Shift** and click the **backdrop-gradient** layer on all the posters to select them all at once and apply the style.

Next, the movie cards. Select the **title** layer and change the fill to **text/secondary**.

Repeat the same process for the three text labels inside the **movie-info** group.

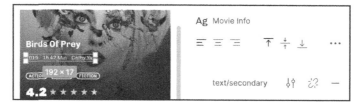

In a moment, you'll tackle the genre and ratings in their component frame. For now, repeat the process and change the fill of the text layers inside the **movie card/ rounded** component.

Then, change the fill style for the **genres** text in the **genres** component.

You also need to change the fill for the enclosing Auto Layout frames.

Styling the icons

Before tackling the navigation component, take a moment to work with the icons. Select the individual icon paths in the **Icons** frame.

Give them a fill style of **navigation/inactive**.

Now, in the **bottom-nav** component, select the **trending** icon and its text label and change their fill to **navigation/active**.

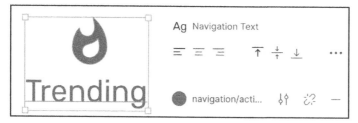

Repeat the same process for the text labels for each navigation target.

For the final piece of the **Components** page, change the **rating** component text's fill to **text/secondary**.

Finally, apply the relevant **rating/positive** fill to the stars.

Updating the details screen

Great job with the styles so far. Since the app uses components in most places, Figma will make a good chunk of the changes automatically. You only need to change the app's details screen.

Open the **Cinematic App** page and, in the **movie-details** frame, change:

- The **title text** color to **text/primary**.

- The **movie-info text** color to **text/muted**.

- All **section header text** colors to **text/primary**.

- The **synopsis text** color to **text/primary**.

- All **user rating text** color to **text/muted**.

- The **button text** color to **text/secondary**.

- The **button fill** to **button/primary**.

After all the modifications are in place, your screens will finally look like this:

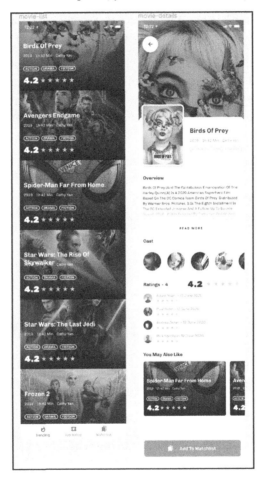

Advantages of color styles

After all that work, none of the visuals in the app have changed. However, you've introduced flexibility that allows you to change the palette and, in turn, the app's styling — without impacting the rest of the design.

This is a great time to use an analogy from engineering. Engineers often practice separation of concerns to reduce tight coupling within their projects. By isolating functionality into separate layers, you reduce the scope of change when you make modifications. This also ensures you don't unknowingly break existing functionality.

You reap those benefits by keeping your styling — i.e., typography and colors — decoupled from your design. When you broke designs into components in the previous chapter, you saw how straightforward it is to switch things around when you needed to. By creating text and color styles, you can make more granular changes to those components with the same advantages.

Congratulations, you've done a great job with the design so far. The screens look appealing and, more importantly, you've laid the groundwork to make future modifications less time-consuming.

In the next chapter, you'll bring these screens to life by adding animations and transitions.

Key points

- You learned the basics of color theory and its importance in design.
- Then you learned about the importance of contrast in design for accessibility.
- You created color styles for the UI elements of the app.
- You then applied the color styles to the components.
- Finally, you learned about the benefits of using reusable styles.

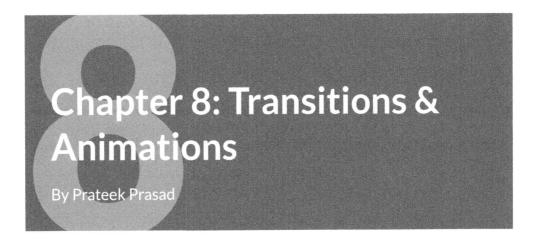

Chapter 8: Transitions & Animations

By Prateek Prasad

In the last chapter, you built a typographic scale and a color palette that helped you decompose your design into even smaller granular layers. You ended the chapter by leveraging these elements in your design and finalized the look of the app.

While the app looks great right now, it's far from finished. Visual appeal is only a part of a great product's story. How it feels and how it's perceived by users are two other important aspects as well.

Static designs like the ones you've created thus far communicate how the app looks. To communicate how it feels to use the app, however, you need to make it interactive.

Interactive prototypes make your designs functional, even though there's no business logic backing them. Prototypes play an essential role in validating functionality and gaining feedback because it lets you put a simple version of your app in real users' hands. The're an inexpensive way to identify friction points in an app's flow and smooth out any rough edges before kicking off the engineering work.

Without user feedback and usability studies, it's entirely possible that your end product won't be usable. Changing things around after a production rollout incurs a considerable cost, in both engineering time and money.

In this chapter, you'll add interactivity and animations to the static screens you finalized in the previous chapter. While you played with Figma's prototyping tools briefly in Chapter 1, "Book Overview & App Preview", you'll now explore Figma's prototyping and animations capability at a deeper level.

Previewing the finished version

If this were the Harry Potter universe, you could see the animations on this page instead of just static images. but sadly it isn't. Some creativity will help, however. Instead of using the final version of this chapter's project as a mere reference, you'll start by examining it.

Doing so will give you a sense of what you'll build and how it should feel in the end.

So far, everything has centered around the app's cosmetic looks so you could rely on the images. However, it's impossible to convey the transitions of animations in print.

Loading the final project

From the downloaded materials, open **chapter-8-final.fig** in Figma. This file has a new page called **Cinematic App Prototype** that contains an interactive version of the app.

> **Note**: Make sure you download the **final** project this time, rather than starting with the starter project. Throughout the chapter, you'll update the starter to match the final version.

This is a separate page because often, while creating prototypes and interactions between different screens, you need to duplicate frames with minor differences to assist in the animation. Sometimes, you'll need to change the contents of a frame or add additional elements to achieve the desired effect. Having a separate copy rather than modifying the original designs will let you change and tweak things without worrying about messing up the final version.

Another reason why you should keep static versions separate is that they are used for developer handoff and exports. Keeping them free of unwanted elements makes the process less confusing.

Ready to get started? Open **Cinematic App Prototype** and click the **Present** button in the toolbar at the top.

This will open up a new tab with the design loaded into an **iPhone 11 Pro Max** frame.

Play around with the prototype. If you're not sure which elements are interactive, click anywhere outside the device frame and the interactive elements will blink, prompting you to click them.

Breaking down the transitions

Now that you've checked out the final app, notice the following transitions in the prototype:

- The transition between the three targets in the bottom navigation.

- The transition from the movie list to the movie Details screen.

- The transition between the **Add to Watchlist** and **Mark Watched** selection state in the Details screen.

If you missed any of them, go back into the prototype and check out their flow and behavior.

First, you'll add the navigation between these states and then you'll add transitions to make them visually appealing.

Loading the starter project

From the downloaded materials, open **chapter-8-starter.fig** in Figma. Open the **Cinematic App Prototype** page. For this chapter, you'll just work in this page.

Setting up the first navigation

Notice that there are two frames on this page: **movie-list-trending** and **movie-details**. For your first step, you'll work on the navigation to bring you from the movie list screen to the movie details screen.

From the **movies-list-trending** frame, expand the **movies** Auto Layout frame and select the **Birds of Prey** instance.

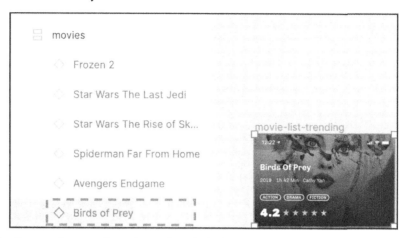

From the Properties panel on the right, click the **Prototype** option.

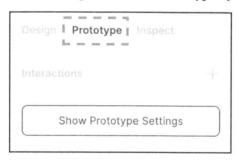

A + button will appear on the right side of the selected instance when you hover over it. Click it and drag it towards the **movie-details** frame to create a link.

An **Interaction Details** pop-up will appear, telling you what will trigger the transition. Leave it to the defaults for now, as shown below:

The **Interaction Details'** default values define that when user clicks the **Birds of Prey** instance, the **movie-details** frame will load without any animations.

In the **movie-details** frame, select **back-button** and add a link back to the **movie-list-trending** frame.

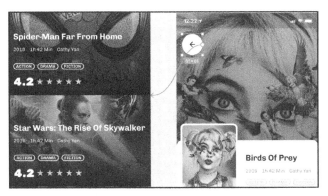

Leave the **Interaction Details** value at the defaults.

Testing your results

It's time to check if things work as you expect. Click the **Present** button on the toolbar at the top of the screen. A new window will open with the screens loaded inside an **iPhone 11 Pro Max** device frame.

Click the "Birds of Prey" movie and you'll navigate into the details screen. Clicking the **Back** button will bring you back to the movie list screen.

But there's a small issue: The navigation bar scrolls along with the list instead of being anchored to the screen's bottom.

To fix this, go back to the editor and click the **Design** tab.

Now, select the **bottom-nav** instance and, under the **Constraints** section, check the **Fix position when scrolling** option.

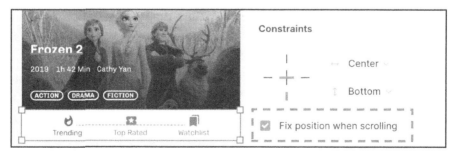

Click the **Present** button again. This time, the bottom navigation stays anchored to the screen's bottom while the list is scrollable.

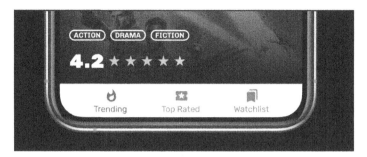

Handling the Add to Watchlist button

Next, you need to handle the **Add to Watchlist** button state. When the user clicks the button:

• The text should say **Mark Watched**.

• The button color should be **button/secondary**.

• The icon of the button should change to **remove_red_eye_24px**.

First, duplicate the **movie-details** screen. Do this by either selecting the **movie-details** frame and pressing **Command/Control-D** or simply copy-pasting with **Command/Control-C** then **Command/Control-V**.

Rename the frame to **movie-details-mark-watched**.

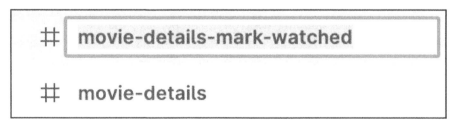

Expand the **add-to-watchlist-button** group and select the **button-background** layer.

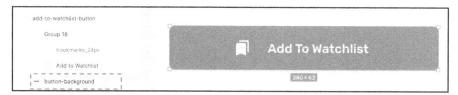

Change the **button-background** layer's fill style to **button/secondary**.

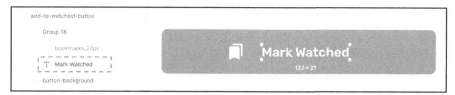

Change the button's text to **Mark Watched**.

Finally, to change the button's icon, select the icon instance from the Layers panel.

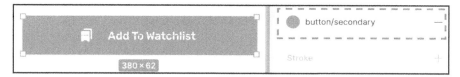

Then, from the instance swapping menu on the Properties panel, select the **remove_red_eye_24px** icon.

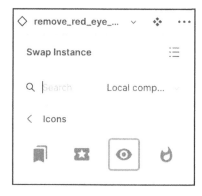

You also need to change the icon color to **text/secondary**.

Finally, rename the group from **add-to-watchlist buttton** to **mark-watched-button**.

Great job! Now, it's time to wire up the navigation to this screen.

Wiring up the navigation

For your first step, select the **add-to-watchlist-button** in the **movie-details** frame and create a link to the **movie-details-mark-watched** frame.

Check the **Preserve scroll position** option — it ensures that when you transition to the next screen, your screen's scroll position stays the same. If the option is unchecked, when you click the button, the next screen will jump back to the top.

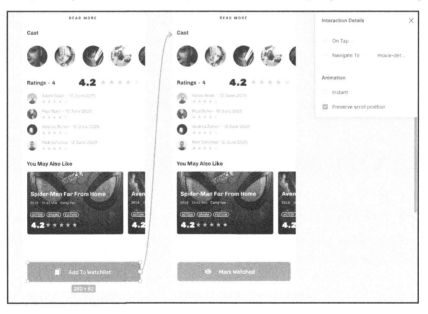

Next, select the **mark-watched-button** and create a link back to the **movie-details** frame. As before, check the **Preserve scroll position** option

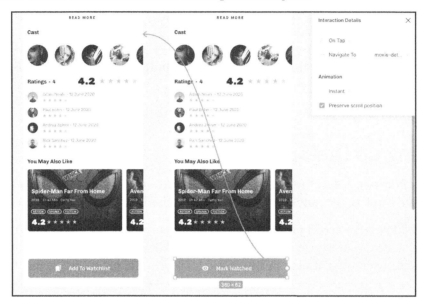

If you head back into the interactive prototype tab and press the button, it will now change states.

Great stuff! Now that you have a basic navigational flow from the list screen to the details screen, it's time to start working on the bottom navigation.

Making the bottom navigation interactive

Since there are three tabs, you'll need three navigational destinations. The trending tab already exists, but you need to add the top-rated and watchlist tabs.

Duplicate **movie-list-trending** twice and rename the new instances to **movie-list-top-rated** and **movie-list-watchlist**.

Instead of adding a new set of movies, all you need to do is shuffle the movies list.

To shuffle the list items, select a list item and drag it up or down to change its position. Here's the list order that the final project uses, for reference:

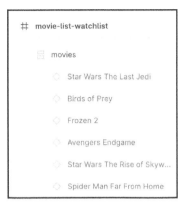

Next, you need to change the active tab on each frame. First, in the **movie-list-top-rated** frame, expand the **bottom-nav** component and select the **trending** item.

Change its fill style to **navigation/inactive**.

Now, select the **top-rated** item and change its fill style to **navigation/active**.

Great job! Now, repeat this process in the **movie-list-watchlist** frame. Change the **trending** item's fill style to **navigation/inactive** and make the watchlist item's fill style **navigation/active**.

Now, you need to wire the navigation items together.

Wiring up the navigation elements

Start with the **movie-details-trending** frame. Select the **top-rated** item in the **bottom-nav** component and create a link to the **movie-list-top-rated** frame.

Then select the **watchlist** item and create a link to the **movie-list-watchlist** frame.

Next, in the **movie-list-top-rated** frame:

- Select the **trending** item in the **bottom-nav** component and create a link to the **movie-list-trending** frame.

- Select the **watchlist** item and create a link to the **movie-list-watchlist** frame.

Finally, in the **movie-list-watchlist** frame:

- Select the **trending** item in the **bottom-nav** component and create a link to the **movie-list-trending** frame.

- Select the **top-rated** item and create a link to the **movie-list-top-rated** frame.

Now, click **Present** and interact with the prototype. You'll be able to click on the navigation targets and to switch between the different screens.

Awesome job! You now have a basic prototype that you can use to navigate the different screens in the app and visualize the different selection states of the buttons in the details UI.

Functionally, the prototype is ready, but it lacks visual appeal; the transitions feel bland. In the next section, you'll fix that by adding animations to make the app extra awesome.

Animations & animation interpolators

Before you move on to adding animations to the prototype, take a moment to understand what animations are and which interpolation options Figma provides.

It's easy to confuse the terms **transitions** and **animations**. Transitions work on a scene or state level and influence larger changes like moving from one screen to another, whereas animations work on an individual element level.

Animations and motion, in general, have a huge influence on how users perceive an app. Besides adding aesthetic flair, animations have other implications, like adding context to what's happening in the app. They help users navigate the app more effortlessly.

Good animations and thoughtfully choreographed motion also help establish visual hierarchy and convey the relationship between different screens to the users. In this app's case, the list screen is the parent, while the details screen is the child, conveying more detail about a selected movie.

When done right, motion can be a useful tool in user education, subtly conveying critical information or feedback on specific actions. A great example of this is the iOS lock screen. When you enter an incorrect passcode, the passcode field wiggles to let you know.

At their essence, animations are just mathematical equations that influence a value — like position, rotation, scale etc. — over time.

These equations, also known as **interpolators**, determine how the animation looks.

Understanding interpolators is key to deciding which animation works best for your specific needs. There's no defined set of rules one can follow to add animations. It boils down to trying and seeing what works best — and, most importantly, what feels right.

Since this is a book where images can't physically move, you'll rely on math and a basic understanding of graphs to understand these concepts.

The graph explaining interpolators has time on the X-axis, which increases from left to right, and the position value on the Y-axis, which increases from the bottom up.

> **Note:** Interpolators are not limited to modifying position values — you can also use them to modify the rotation scale and other attributes. This chapter focuses on position values because they're easier to imagine.

Types of interpolators

Before you start adding animations to the Cinematic app, take a moment to learn about the different types of interpolators Figma offers.

Linear interpolator

The first interpolator you will look at is **linear**. Linear interpolation is represented as a straight line, meaning the change in position is linearly related to the change in time:

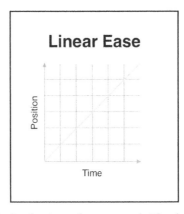

Linear movements often feel robotic and unnatural. That's because, in the real world, all movement is influenced by inertia.

Objects don't suddenly start and stop, they start slowly and accelerate or decelerate until they stop.

Ease-in interpolator

In an **ease-in** curve, as shown in the graph, changes in an object's position start slowly and accelerate as time passes. Their quickest rate of motion is at the end of the animation. Imagine, for example, a car stopped at a traffic light. When the light turns green, the car accelerates away.

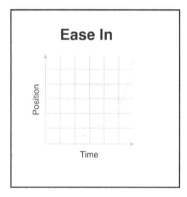

Ease-in interpolation is an excellent choice for moving elements off the screen.

Ease-out interpolator

An **ease-out** curve is the opposite of an ease-in curve, as shown in the graph below. Changes in the object's position start fast and slow down toward the end of the animation. For example, imagine a cartoon character running in and skidding to a stop.

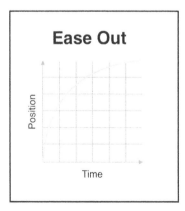

Ease-out interpolation works well for moving elements into the screen.

Ease-in-and-out interpolator

An **ease-in-and-out** interpolator starts the interpolation slowly, accelerating in the middle and slowing down towards the end. A good example is a sprinter who starts from a fixed position, runs the race, and then slows to a stop after the finish line.

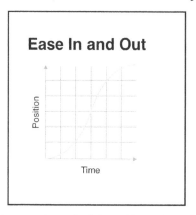

This interpolation makes interactions feel friendly and perfect — but overusing it can lead to transitions feeling oddly unnatural.

Ease-in-back interpolator

The **ease-in-back** interpolator starts by moving the object back a few positions, then releasing it to accelerate toward the end, like when you draw a pinball plunger back before releasing the ball. This is useful when you need anticipation in your animations or want to create bouncy -or springy- feeling animations.

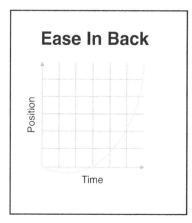

When used tastefully, it adds a flare of fun to the animations.

Ease-out-back interpolator

The **ease-out-back** interpolator is the opposite of the ease-in-back interpolator. It starts by accelerating the object, then moves the object past the final position before arriving at the final position. Imagine dropping a heavy ball onto a stretchy surface, where it drops below the surface then springs back to rest upon it.

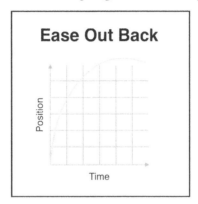

The ease-out-back interpolator gives the animations a bounce or a reactionary motion. You can use this as a subtle ending to an animation.

Ease-in-and-out-back interpolator

The **ease-in-and-out-back** interpolator combines the ease-in-back interpolator and the ease-out-back interpolator. It creates an anticipatory backward-bounce motion at the beginning, an acceleration in the middle, and then a bounce towards the end.

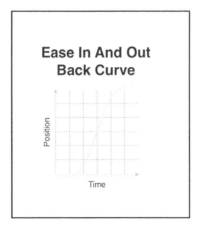

Now that you've covered what interpolators are and how they influence values, it's time to get started with the animation for navigating between the list screen and the details screen.

Implementing the navigation animations

The animations in the final project have four key aspects:

- The backdrop grows and increases in opacity from the middle of the screen.

- The details screen image grows and moves up to its final position.

- The title, movie info, genres, overview and background cards move up to their final positions from the bottom of the screen.

- The **Back** button grows to its final size in its final position.

To see this in action, open the final project's interactive prototype and test it out.

To achieve the final effect, you'll use a clever feature in Figma called **Smart Animate**.

Using Smart Animate

Smart Animate takes a starting state and a final state for an element and animates the element's properties between those two states. If you've used Keynote's Magic Move feature, Smart Animate works the same way, just for your Figma designs.

There are two requirements to get Smart Animate to work properly:

- The element that you need to animate must exist on both the starting screen and the final screen.

- The element must have the same name on both the starting screen and the final screen.

These requirements are very important to keep in mind. If even one of these is violated, you'll end up with a weird or broken animation.

> **Note:** Smart Animate is very similar to using **Shared Element Transitions** on Android. The underlying mechanics are also very similar. The shared element transition animates a view between its starting and final state provided the view is present on both screens and has the same tag in both layout XML files.

Start with a simple example, to get the hang of Smart Animate.

Animating the Back button

When you enter the details screen, the **Back** button should grow from a point size to its final form.

To make this happen, copy the **back-button** in the **movie-details** frame and paste it into the **movie-list-trending** frame.

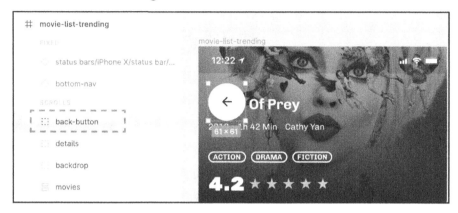

This will copy the button in the same position as in the details screen.

Select the **back-button** you just copied and:

- Change the **width** and **height** to **1**.

- Change the **X** value to **36** and the **Y** value to **70**.

- Change the **opacity** to **0%**.

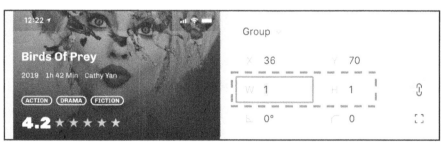

> **Note**: If you lose the selection because the button is too small to manipulate directly with your mouse, just select **back-button** from the Layers panel and modify its properties.

All right, now you need to make one final change so you can preview this animation.

Go into the **Prototype** section and select the link you added from the "Birds of Prey" movie to the details screen. Under the **Animation** section, select **Smart Animate** from the drop-down. Use **Ease In And Out** as the interpolator and specify a **duration** of **600ms**.

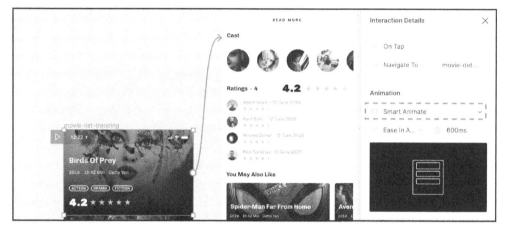

Time for some fun. Click on the **Present** button and click the **Birds of Prey** movie card. You'll see the **Back** button grows from a small point into its full size.

For a little test, rename the **back-button** on the **movie-list-trending** frame to **back-button-2** and try interacting with the prototype. You'll see it no longer works. Be sure to change the name back before proceeding.

To stress this point again, ensure the elements you are trying to animate:

- Exist on both frames.

- Have the same names on both frames.

Animating the details card

Next, you need the details card to slide up into place when the user enters the details screen.

To do so, first, copy the **details** group from the **movie-details** frame to the **movie-list-trending** frame.

As you saw earlier, the copied group will maintain its position.

Select the **details** group you copied and change the **Y** value to **923**.

Next, expand the **details** group and select the **title**, **movie-info**, **genre**, **overview-header** and the **overview-text** layers and group them (**G**).

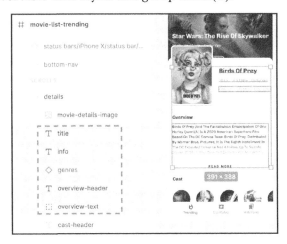

Name the group **details-animated-content**.

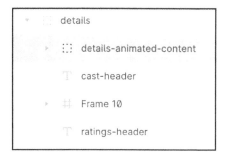

Select the **details-animated-content** group and change the **X** value to **16** and the **Y** value to **1091**.

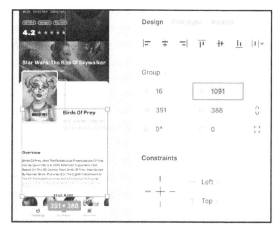

Reduce its opacity to 50% by setting the **Layer Pass Through** to **50.**.

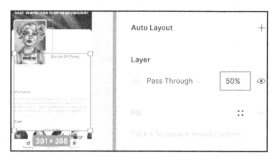

Next, the image. Select the **movie-details-image** in **movie-list-trending** screen and:

• Change **X** to **73** and **Y** to **1031**.

- Change the **width** and **height** to **10**.

Finally, change the **fill opacity** and the **stroke opacity** to **0%**.

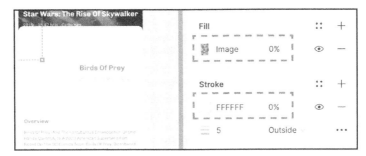

For your last step, select the **details** group in the **movie-list-trending** frame and change the opacity to **0%**.

Click the **Present** button and view the prototype. You'll notice the details section and the **Back** button animate into their final positions when you click the "Birds of Prey" movie card.

You can see that a lot of what you did to achieve this effect was smoke and mirrors. Smart Animate works on a simple premise of interpolating values between the initial and final state. Everything you make the tool do in between is trickery — and magic, in a way.

Animating the backdrop

You're almost there with the effect. You just need to add one last bit to wrap it up, which is animating the backdrop.

In the final project, the backdrop image grows to its final size from the screen's center. You'll add that animation now.

First, copy the **backdrop** group from the **movie-details** screen and paste it into the **movie-list-trending** frame.

Select the **backdrop** layer you copied and change the **width** to **399** and the **height** to **991**.

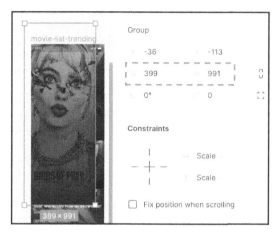

Next, align the **backdrop** layer **horizontally** and **vertically** in the frame. You can use the alignment options from the **Design** section.

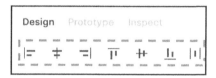

Now, select the **backdrop** layer and, from the **Effects** section, give it a **Layer Blur** with a value of **90**.

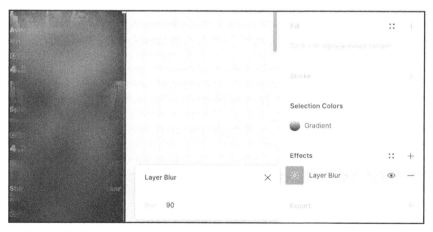

Finally, change the layer's **opacity** to **0%**.

Click the **Present** button now and interact with the prototype. The details screen animates into the screen beautifully. The button grows in place, and the backdrop and details group expand from the bottom of the screen.

Animating the transition to the list screen

You need to tweak one final thing to complete the animation: When you click the **Back** button on the details screen, there's no transition when you return to the list screen.

Ideally, the animations should play in reverse when you click the **Back** button and exit the details screen. With Smart Animate, this is relatively straightforward to do.

Return to the editor and click the **Prototype** option. Now, select the link from the **Back** button on the **movie-details** frame to the **movie-list-trending** frame.

Change the animation to **Smart Animate**, use the **Ease Out** interpolator. And give it a duration of **400 ms**.

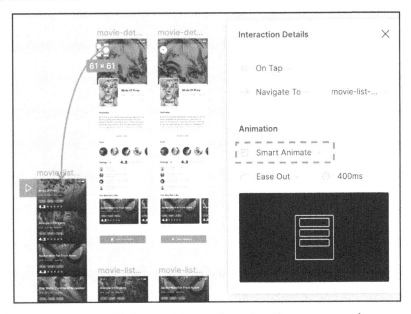

Now, when you interact with the prototype, the animation reverses when you exit the details screen.

Using animations thoughtfully

Great job building a fully interactive prototype! Even with the minimal set of prototyping options available in Figma, you can create sophisticated and slick-looking animations and transitions.

Now is a great time to quote Uncle Ben: "With great power comes great responsibility."

Since Figma abstracts away a lot of the underlying grunt work to make your animations work, its simplified toolset can create some really complex looking custom animations. But you don't necessarily have to create those complex animations, just because they look cool.

Often, when building such transitions, you need to be mindful of the engineering effort it involves to bring them to life. You also need to ask yourself if these transitions help the user in any way, or if they're just adding unnecessary friction.

This finesse will come naturally with time as you create more designs, do user testing and gather feedback. For now, the prototypes you just created strike the right balance between being visually pleasing and being straightforward enough to replicate in code.

In the next chapter, you'll learn how to share your designs with your team, gather feedback and add some final polish.

Key points

- You learned about the basics of transitions and animations.

- You learned about animation interpolators and the different interpolators available in Figma.

- You created links between the different screens and the bottom navigation targets.

- You explored the Smart Animate feature in Figma.

- You used Smart Animate to create a sophisticated-looking animation from the list screen to the details screen.

Chapter 9: Feedback & Testing

By Prateek Prasad

You finished the last chapter with a fully functional prototype that not only looks great but also supports interaction. You're now at a critical checkpoint in the design lifecycle. At this point, your designs are detailed enough to communicate the core intent and you've structured your workspace so that introducing new additions or making changes to existing pieces won't be a massive undertaking.

Now, it's time to put the designs into the hands of users and stakeholders, get feedback and brainstorm about what you can improve. The importance of cross-team collaboration is a point I have been stressing over the previous chapters. Now, it's finally time to put it into practice.

This chapter will show you another reason behind picking Figma as the design tool of choice.

So far, you've explored two of the three pillars of what makes Figma an excellent design tool:

1. Minimal toolset with powerful features that make translating ideas into design easy.

2. Built-in prototyping tools allow you to bring your designs to life with minimal effort.

The third pillar is rich collaboration tools that make asynchronous communication and collaboration in a distributed setting painless.

For designers who need to go from wireframes to high-fidelity designs to a fully interactive prototype, these features are compelling. They not only eliminate the need to learn and switch between three tools to close the product development loop, but they also improve productivity by leaps and bound.

This chapter is all about collaboration. The three key things you'll learn are how to:

- Prep your files and prototypes and share them with stakeholders.

- Gather feedback and suggestions.

- Incorporate feedback into the designs.

Now, it's time to get started.

From the downloaded materials, open **chapter-9-starter.fig** in Figma.The project file contains the prototype, wireframes and designs in their final form.

In this chapter, you'll work with the **Cinematic App** design and the **Cinematic App Prototype**.

Soliciting feedback

When you build a new product, getting feedback early and often is key to ensuring you're on the right track. Without feedback, it's easy to get sidetracked and build something completely different from the original idea.

Feedback brings diverse perspectives into the design process and helps build inclusive and accessible products.

Typically, when gathering feedback, you want to include both the internal teams involved in building the products and the users or customers who'll use the app.

Internal teams can bring their ideas and constraints to the table early on. Involving real users lets you observe any friction points in their interaction with the product. Ideally, this happens frequently and in different stages of development, offering you the opportunity to correct your course while the designs and ideas are still flexible enough to change.

It's also worth mentioning that nothing is set in stone when figuring out how to best collaborate with all stakeholders. The right method depends on factors like the structure of your teams, how communication works in the organization and the test group's availability.

Now that you know why collaboration is so important, it's time to prepare the prototype so you can share it with other teammates and pass it on for user testing.

Preparing the prototype for testing

Open the **Cinematic App Prototype** page. You need to check a few things before passing it along to others, including:

- The prototype uses an appropriate device frame.

- The prototype works as expected.

- The link to access the prototype works and you've enabled the correct permissions.

You'll start with the frame.

Checking the prototype's frame

First, click on the **Prototype** tab on the Properties panel and ensure you've selected the **iPhone 11 Pro Max** under **Device**.

Adding a device frame to a prototype gives your testers a better idea of what the app will look like on a real device when it's finished.

Figma lets you change the prototype's background to suit your presentation arrangement, but for now, you'll keep the default: black.

Next, in the **Prototype** section, check that you've set **movie-list-trending** as the starting frame.

This ensures that viewers who interact with the prototype have the right starting point in the app flow.

Now that you've checked these two settings, you're ready to share the prototype.

Sharing the prototype

Click the **Present** button to open the prototype in a separate tab, then click **Share Prototype**. The dialog that appears lets you modify the access controls.

If you're a part of a Figma team, all team members have access to the prototype — and the design files — by default.

Before anyone outside the team can access the prototype, you need to invite them. To ensure that people outside the team can't make any unwanted modifications to the designs, change the access control to **can view**.

Another way to share prototypes is to create a shareable link. Click **Anyone with the link** in the share options, then click **Copy link**. This will copy the link to the prototype to your clipboard.

Before sharing the link, check that it works. A quick way is to open the link inside an incognito browser window. If the prototype loads as expected, the link works.

Sharing the design files

The prototype gives stakeholders an idea of what using the app feels like. However, to gather more fine-grained feedback about the design, such as the color palette and typography, you need to share the design files.

To do so, head to the **Cinematic App** page and click the **Share** button in the toolbar. The resulting share options dialog is similar to the one you used to share the prototype.

When you share the designs with other designers in the team, you probably want to allow them to make modifications. To do so, change the share setting to **Only people invited to this file** and select the **can edit** option for the email of each person you invite to the file.

> **Note**: Figma's free plan only allows two users to have edit access to a file, which should be enough for most side projects. To add more editors to a file, you need to upgrade to a paid plan.

Great job. You've now learned how to share your designs and prototypes with others so they can give you their thoughts and suggestions. Before proceeding, you'll look at how to change the access controls for users you've already invited.

Moderating access

Moderating access to files is handy for revoking access for someone who is no longer a part of the project or modifying the access controls for existing viewers and editors.

To change the access rights for the design file, click the **Share** button to bring up the share menu. Here, you can edit the access controls for existing viewers and editors.

If needed, you can remove viewers and editors from the files by selecting the **Remove** option from the drop-down.

To modify the prototype's access controls, click the **Present** button to open the prototype in a separate tab. Then, click the **Share Prototype** button to bring up the share menu. The options to modify viewers' access and remove them are the same as those you used to modify access for the design files.

Leaving feedback on design files

Before you incorporate feedback into your designs, consider how you can leave feedback and suggestions to get a 360-degree view of the process. Figma comes with a handy **Comment** option that you can find on the toolbar or activate by pressing **C**.

This changes your mouse pointer to a marker you can place anywhere in the design file. When you place the marker on the design by clicking the canvas, a dialog box will open. This allows you to leave comments, feedback or suggestions.

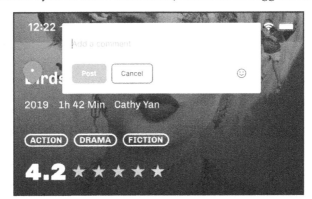

Incorporating feedback

Now, imagine that you've shared the file and prototypes with your team and the test group. It's now time to incorporate their feedback into your designs.

Depending on your team's preferences and set processes, you can use different tools and platforms to collate and track feedback. Still, the essence of the feedback process tends to stay the same.

In this hypothetical scenario, the design has received two pieces of feedback.

One comes from an actual user who interacted with the prototype:

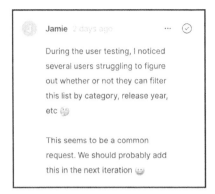

The other comes from an internal stakeholder:

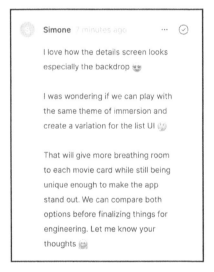

If you recall, you built a filter feature in the chapter on wireframing. However, you never actually designed the feature — showing what happens if you don't tackle critical use cases and iron out functional constraints during wireframing. In this case, user testing and feedback acted as a safety net, letting you address the point of friction in a user's flow.

Imagine if you just went ahead designing the app according to your assumptions without involving others in the decisions and without feedback from the end-user. You'd still have a good looking app, but it would have some massive functional flaws.

That's why collaboration, testing and feedback are essential elements of a great design team's workflow. They not only help you build a better, more inclusive product but also give you a broader perspective into the problem you're solving.

First, you'll work on the filter feature. When that's done, you'll tackle the movie list iteration.

Designing the filter feature

The filter feature allows users to filter the main feed by:

- Genres

- Release year

- Director

- Duration

Adding a launch button

First, you'll add a button to launch the filter UI. Open the **Cinematic App** page and, in the **movie-list** frame, add an ellipse (**O**) measuring **60×60** with a white fill. Place it above **bottom-nav** at a margin of **32** fromthe right and bottom.

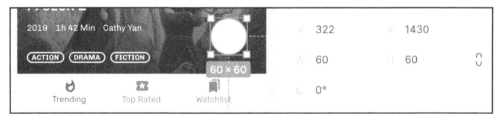

Next, from the assets, add the **filter_list_24px** icon above the circle and center the icon both **vertically** and **horizontally** within the circle.

Group the circle and the icon and name it **filter-button**.

Constrain this group to the bottom and right and check the **Fix position when scrolling** option.

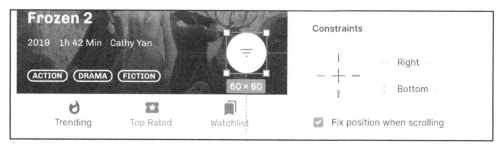

To check that the button stays anchored to the bottom when scrolling, click the **Present** button to open the prototype. When you scroll the movie list, the button stays in its location.

Building the filter UI

Next, you'll handle the filter UI. Before building the filter sheet, you'll build each component for the individual filter criteria.

Open the **Typography** page and add a new text layer (**T**) below the **Genre Text** layer and add the text: **Filter Text**.

Use the font **Rubik** with a weight of **Medium** and a font size of **12**.

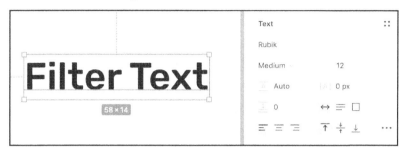

Keeping the layer selected, click the **Style** button, and create a new text style. Name it **Filter Text**.

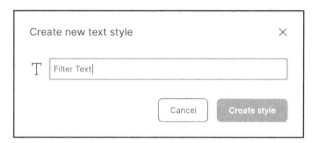

Next, open the **Components** page and create a new frame (**F**) measuring **242×92** and name it **Filter**.

Add a new text layer (**T**) to this frame with the text **Action**. Use the newly created **Filter Text** text style for this layer.

With the layer selected, press **Shift-A** to create an Auto Layout frame from the text layer. Name it **criteria**.

From the **Stroke** section of the Properties panel, give the criteria frame a stroke of width **2** using the color style **text/accent**. Make sure you apply the stroke to the **Center**.

Change the criteria frame's corner radius to **5**.

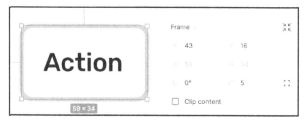

Next, from the Auto Layout properties section, click the **Alignment and padding** option.

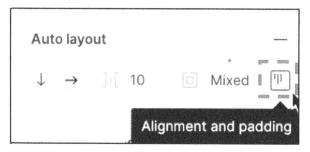

Change the **Horizontal padding** to **8** and the **Vertical Padding** to **2**.

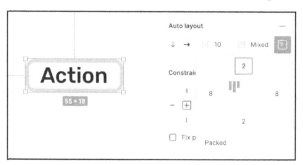

Finally, change the text color to use the **text/accent** color style.

Duplicate the criteria frame to the right with a margin of **8** and change the text to **Drama**.

Repeat the process once more, changing the text to **Fiction**. Group the three criteria frames and name the group **Filter/Unchecked**.

You'll need a checked variant of the filter criteria as well.

Instead of building it from scratch, duplicate the **Filter/Unchecked** group and rename it to **Filter/Checked**.

Expand the group and select the three criteria frames, then remove the stroke.

Add a fill to the three frames using the **text/accent** color style.

The text is hidden at this point. To fix it, select the individual text elements in the group and change the color style to **text/secondary**.

Select **Filter/Unchecked** and create an Auto Layout frame (**Shift-A**). Give it horizontal and vertical padding of **0** and item spacing of **8**. Do the same for **Filter/Checked**.

Finally, select the **Filter/Unchecked** frame and create a component by clicking the **Create component** button on the toolbar or selecting the group, right-clicking and choosing the **Create component** option. Do the same for **Filter/Checked**.

Building the filter sheet

To build the filter sheet, open the **Cinematic App** page and duplicate the **movie-list** frame by selecting the frame in the Layers list and pressing **Command-D** or **Control-D**. Name the frame **movie-list-filter** and delete **filter-button** from the frame.

Select the frame and reduce its height to **896**.

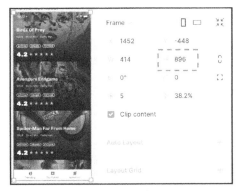

While you're at it, lock the **movie-list**, **bottom-nav** and **status-bar** frames since you don't need to modify them.

Next, add a rectangle (**R**) to the frame measuring **414×448** and place it right above the **bottom-nav**. Give the rectangle a **white** fill and name it **filter-background**.

Apply a **Drop Shadow** from the **Effects** options to the **filter-background** with **X** and **Y** set to **0**.

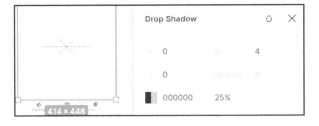

Add a text layer (**T**) on top of the **filter-background** layer and give it the text **Genres**. Apply the **Section Header** text style to this layer and name the layer **genres-filter**.

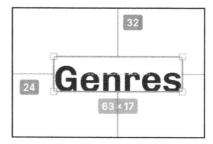

Place it at a margin of **32** from the top and **24** from the left.

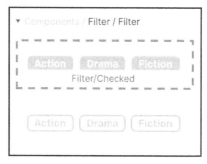

Next, from the **Assets** section, add a **Filter/Checked** instance below the Genres text layer.

Place it at a margin of **16** from the top and **24** from the left.

Adding the genres

Duplicate the instance and place it to the right at a margin of **8**. Change the text of the criteria frames to **Scifi**, **Period** and **Romance**.

Swap the component to **Filter/Unchecked**.

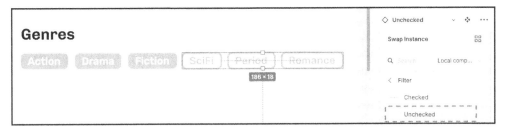

Duplicate the unchecked criteria row and place it at the bottom of the checked row. Give it a margin of **12** from the top and **24** from the right. Change the criteria text to **Thriller**, **Horror** and **Mystery**.

For the final criteria, add another **Filter/Unchecked** instance to the right at a margin of **8** and change the first criteria to **Musical**. Select the other two criteria and hide them.

Now, select the **genres-filter** text and the four filter instances and group them. Name the group **genres-category**.

Adding filter rows

Add another text layer to the bottom of the **genres-category** with the text **Release Year** and **Section Header** text style. Repeat the steps you followed for the genres filter criteria to create the filter rows, as shown below.

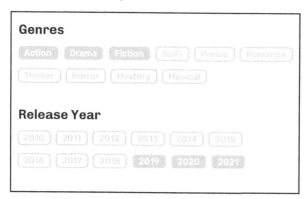

The filter UI will have two more categories, **Directors** and **Duration**. Repeat the steps you followed this far to create these two categories.

As shown below.

Feel free to refer to the final project if you need help.

Finishing up

For the final polish, select the **filter-background** and double-click it to enter the vector editing mode.

Select the **top right** and **top left** corners, hold **Shift** and click each one. Give the selected corners a corner radius of **16**.

Finally, from the **Assets** section, add the **expand_more_24px** icon and place it on the top-right of **filter-background** at a margin of **16** from the **right** and the **top**.

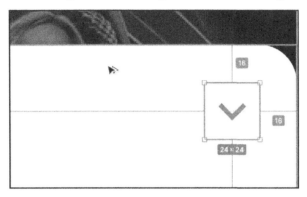

Here's how the final version looks:

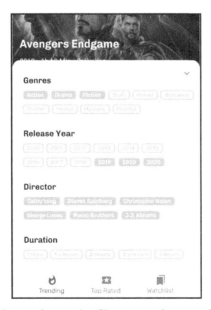

Group all the elements that make up the filter UI and name the group **filter-sheet**.

Constrain the filter-sheet to the **center** and **bottom** and check the **Fix position when scrolling** option.

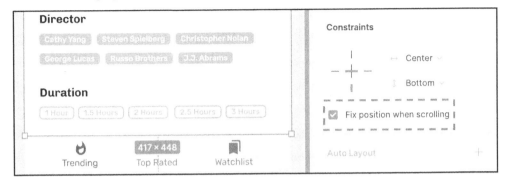

Great job designing the filter UI. You've just solved one of the app's pain points and you've improved the user experience considerably in the process. Next, you'll iterate on the movie list screen and create a new variation to incorporate the PM's suggestion.

Creating the movie list iteration

Your next goal is to tackle the feedback left by one of your teammates. Here's the comment:

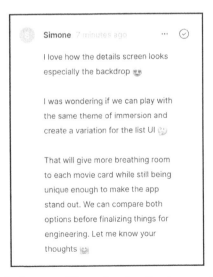

In the new movie list variation, you'll emphasize the immersion aspect of the feedback which will also take care of making the screen stand out more.

To give you a sneak peek, here's what the new version will look like next to the current version.

Lucky for you, the iteration will be relatively quick because of the way you've structured your project so far. You'll leverage components, styles and existing layouts to make your changes.

Inside **Cinematic App**, add a new **iPhone 11 Pro Max** frame (**F**) to the canvas and name it **movie-list-immersive**.

Copy the **backdrop** group from the **movie-details** frame and paste it into the new frame.

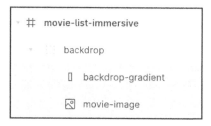

Change the dimension of the backdrop group to **414×896**.

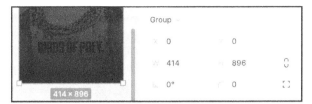

Next, select the **backdrop-gradient** and **movie-image** layers within the group and change their dimension to **414×896**. Center the **backdrop-gradient** and **movie-image** layers **horizontally** and **vertically** and center the **backdrop** layer **horizontally** and **vertically** within the frame.

Here's how the final version should look:

Next, copy the **bottom-nav** and the **status bar** instances from the **movie-list-filter** frame. If you locked them earlier, you'll have to unlock them first. Finally, paste them into the **movie-list-immersive** frame.

The status bar and bottom navigation now retain their positions.

To prevent unintended modifications, lock the **bottom-nav**, **status bar** and **backdrop** layers.

Upgrading the movie card

Now, for the fun part. Create a rectangle (**R**) measuring **300×579** in the frame. If the rectangle isn't visible, check your Layers panel and ensure the rectangle is above the backdrop layer.

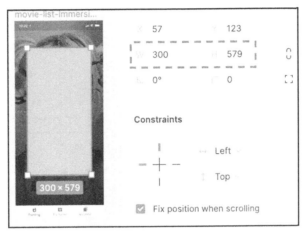

Give the rectangle a corner radius of **24** and a **white** fill and place it below the status bar.

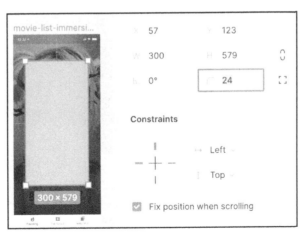

Give it a margin of **80** from the top and center the rectangle **horizontally** using the alignment options on the Properties panel's top. Name this rectangle **movie-card-background**.

Add another rectangle (**R**) measuring **238×343** to the frame, above **movie-card-background**. Give the rectangle a corner radius of **24**.

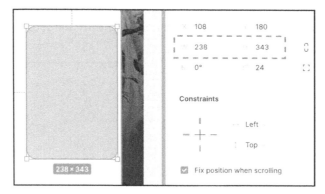

Place it at a margin of **31** from the **top**, **right**, and **left**.

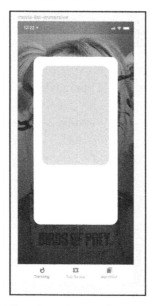

Give this rectangle an **Image** fill. Select the **Birds of Prey** movie poster from the **movie-images** folder that came with the downloaded files.

Name this layer **movie-image**.

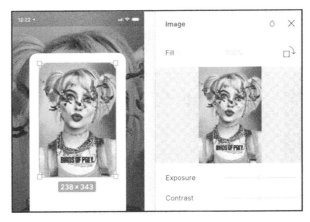

Good going! Next, add a text layer (**T**) to the frame with the text **Birds of Prey**. Place it below the **movie-image** layer at a margin of **20** from the top and apply the **Title** text style. Center the layer **horizontally**. Name the layer **title**.

Now, copy the **movie-info** and **genres** instances from the **movie-details** frame and paste them into the **movie-list-immersive** frame. Center both the layers horizontally.

Place **movie-info** below the **title** layer with a margin of **16** from the top. Place the **genres** instance below the **movie-info** layer with a margin of **16** from the top.

For the final piece, add a **rating** instance below the **genres** instance from the **Assets** section.

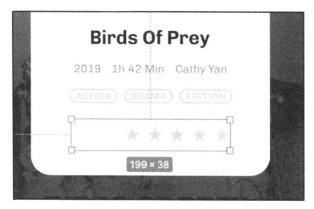

Apply the **text/muted** color style to the rating text and center it **horizontally** with a margin of **20** from the top.

Group all the elements that make up the movie card and name the group **movie-card**.

Adding finishing touches

Finally, to add the finishing touch to this list, duplicate the **movie-card** group towards the **right** at a margin of **42**.

When you do so, the duplicated instance will jump out of the **movie-list-immersive** frame. Notice the same on the Layers panel.

To fix it, in the Layers panel, simply drag the duplicated instance back into the **movie-list-immersive** frame, and you're good to go.

Repeat the same process and duplicate a **movie-card** instance to the left at a margin of **42**. Group the three **movie-card** instances and name the group **movie-list**.

This is how the final version will look:

Great job! The final designs look great at this stage, but more importantly, you've fixed the issues with the functionality and improved the user experience. In the real world, the feedback and testing phase in a design cycle takes more time due to the nature of the process and multiple moving pieces, but this simulated scenario gives you a sense of the process.

Key points

- You learned how to prepare your designs and prototypes for sharing.

- You learned about the different collaboration tools Figma offers.

- You learned how to provide design feedback using the comment tool.

- You then incorporated user feedback to solve a functional issue.

- You finally incorporated an internal suggestion to iterate on the movie list screen and make it more immersive.

In the next chapter, you'll build a design system from the project's different elements and prepare to share it widely within your organization.

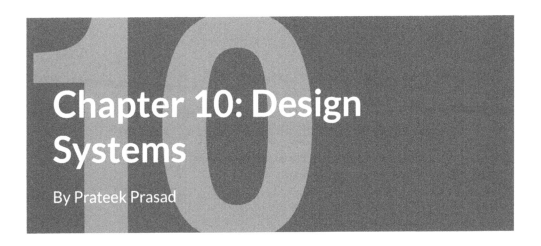

Chapter 10: Design Systems

By Prateek Prasad

Over the course of the past nine chapters, you've gone through an entire design cycle, building out a fully-fledged mobile app experience and picking up the tools of the trade along the way.

You looked at existing apps for inspiration and uncovered their design foundations. You also discovered some neat patterns to address interface challenges, like navigation and forming an informational hierarchy.

Using what you learned, you built out a prototype of your designs and used components to refine it. While you did all that. you also introduced a lot of flexibility in the process.

In this chapter, you'll connect everything you've learned so far to understand how that information comes together in a design system.

Understanding design systems

At its most primitive level, a design system is simply a collection of components you can reuse and recombine to design apps built according to a standard.

Think of those components like Lego bricks, which you can combine in multiple ways to build new experiences.

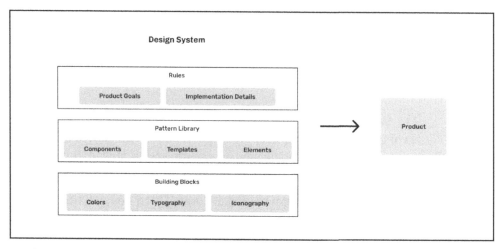

Don't confuse design systems with style guides and UI kits, which are collections of pre-styled templates to use for building screens. They focus on a much higher level of abstraction.

Design systems go much deeper, bringing coherence to an organization's products. Think about it this way: In a large company, multiple designers work on the same product and features. When each designer tackles the project in their own unique way, it results in unwanted variations and inconsistencies in different features of the same product. That becomes confusing for users.

Following a guideline and reusing the same fundamental principles across features and screens brings cohesion and consistency, not only within a single product's features, but also across multiple products offered by the same company.

An analogy that might resonate well with engineers is to think of it like extracting core pieces of business logic into reusable libraries or modules and leveraging them when building new features for your products.

Just like coding convention and style guidelines, how you build a design system varies across different companies and teams to suit their unique needs. The process evolves over time.

Goals of a design system

Although design systems vary dramatically from company to company, there are some common goals they all try to meet:

- **Removing inconsistency**: By breaking designs down to their most fundamental pieces, like reusable text, color styles and components, design systems ensure that the features and experiences you design have a consistent visual look and feel.

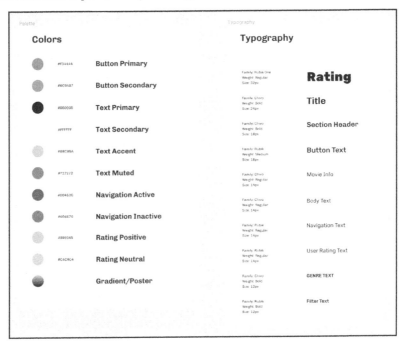

- **Saving time**: By investing once in building reusable components, future iterations become significantly faster than building everything from scratch.

- **Introducing fluidity in the design process**: Design systems are layered and interconnected. You use typography and colors to create components, and you use components to create screens. This layering makes revisions and future tweaks a breeze compared to making a change in multiple places, one at a time.

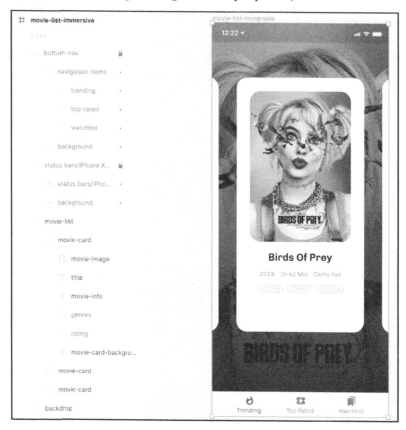

- **Making collaboration and handoff seamless**: By establishing consistency in lower-level details like typography, colors and components, design systems ensure that different teams can work on different parts of a product simultaneously without deviating from the brand's essence.

If you think about these goals for a minute, you might realize that Cinematic, in the state you left it in Chapter 9, "Feedback & Testing", already achieves most of them. You've been building a design system all along! Didn't see that coming? This chapter will zoom out and help you connect the dots.

Cinematic has already decomposed colors and low-level typography details into different pages as reusable styles for your components to use. All it lacks is some cleanup and documentation. You'll fix that next.

Organizing the colors

Download this chapter's materials, then open **chapter-10-starter.fig** in Figma. This file contains the final states of the components, typography and colors. You'll start by organizing and documenting the colors.

Open the **Colors** page. Add a new frame on this page measuring **458×699**. Name the frame **Palette** and give it a fill of **#F1F1F1**. This is where you'll organize your color swatches.

Now, add a new text layer with the text **Colors** and give it a text style of **Title**.

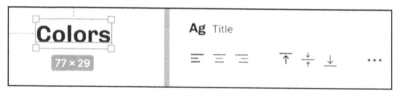

Place this layer at a margin of **16** from the top and **32** from the left.

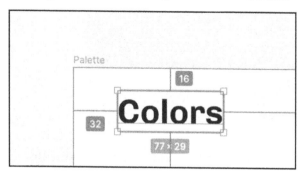

Next, move the circle representing the **button/primary** swatch and place it below the title at a margin of **32** from the top and left.

Now, add a text layer to represent the color's hex code, which you find by clicking the **Edit Style** option next to the color style's name.

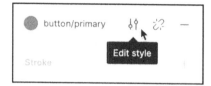

Give this text layer a font size of **9** and use **Chivo-Regular** as the font. Place it at a margin of **36** from the left while aligning it horizontally with the circle.

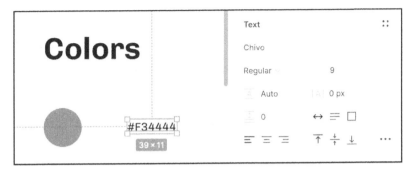

Next, add another text layer to represent the color style name. Use the **Section Header** text style on this layer and place it at a margin of **56** from the left.

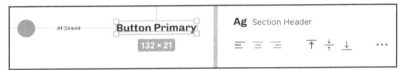

Select the three layers you just added and horizontally align them. For convenience, group them.

Now, move the circle representing the **button/secondary** swatch and place it below the group you just created at a margin of **24** from the top and **32** from the left.

Repeat the steps above to add a text layer for the hex code and another one for the style name.

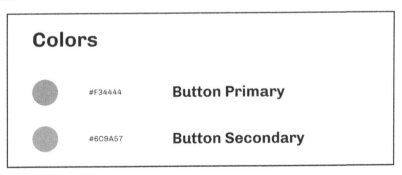

Once done, tackle the remaining nine swatches in the following logical order

- Text Primary

- Text Secondary

- Text Accent

- Text Muted

- Navigation Active

- Navigation Inactive

- Rating Positive

- Rating Neutral

- Gradient Poser

Here's how the final version should look:

Colors

	#F34444	**Button Primary**
	#6C9A57	**Button Secondary**
	#000000	**Text Primary**
	#FFFFFF	**Text Secondary**
	#B9C95A	**Text Accent**
	#727272	**Text Muted**
	#0045D0	**Navigation Active**
	#6D6E70	**Navigation Inactive**
	#89E045	**Rating Positive**
	#C4C4C4	**Rating Neutral**
		Gradient/Poster

Now, delete the old palette artboard. By organizing and documenting your color palette, you've made it easier for your teammates to glance over the colors and their respective hex values. This type of documentation is especially beneficial for engineers, helping them use the correct colors when they build these layouts in code.

Now that you've cleaned up the colors page, you'll tweak the Typography page and make it a bit more informational.

Improving the Typography page

Open the **Typography** page and add a new frame measuring **397×774**.

Next, add a text layer to this frame with the text **Typography** and give it a **Title** text style. Place this layer at a margin of **16** from the top and **32** from the left.

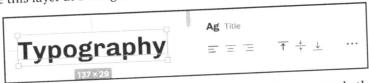

Now, you'll add information about each text style on this frame, namely the:

- Font family

- Font weight

- Font size

Start with the **Rating** text style. Add a new text layer to the frame and enter the **Rating** text style's family weight and font size:

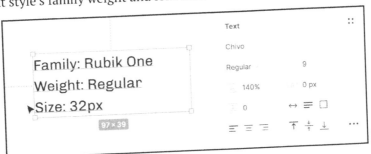

Note: Find information about each text style by clicking the **Edit Style** button in the Properties panel on the right.

Next, place the **Rating** text style to the right of the new text layer at a margin of **68** from the left. Group the two layers.

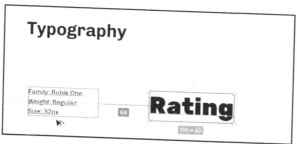

Now, repeat the same for the **Title** text style. Add a new text layer for the style information and place it below the group you created earlier at a margin of **24** from the top and **32** from the left. Feed the style information into the text layer, then place the text style to the right of this layer.

Similarly, tackle the remaining styles. This is how your typography layer will look when you're done:

Typography

Family: Rubik One Weight: Regular Size: 32px	**Rating**
Family: Chivo Weight: Bold Size: 24px	**Title**
Family: Chivo Weight: Bold Size: 18px	**Section Header**
Family: Rubik Weight: Medium Size: 18px	**Button Text**
Family: Chivo Weight: Regular Size: 14px	Movie Info
Family: Chivo Weight: Regular Size: 14px	Body Text
Family: Rubik Weight: Regular Size: 14px	Navigation Text
Family: Rubik Weight: Regular Size: 14px	User Rating Text
Family: Chivo Weight: Bold Size: 12px	**GENRE TEXT**
Family: Rubik Weight: Bold Size: 12px	**Filter Text**

The typographic scale is now much more informational. The documentation eliminates the need for other teammates to inspect each style manually to figure out its specifics.

Cleaning up the Components page

For the final bit of cleanup, open the **Components** page. There are a few things to improve here.

First, the icons. The names of the icons and the context in which they've been used in the project are confusing.

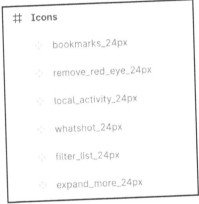

You'll fix that now. Change the name of the icons as follows:

- **bookmarks_24px** to **icon-watchlist**
- **remove_red_eye_24px** to **icon-watched**
- **local_activity_24px** to **icon-top-rated**
- **whatshot_24px** to **icon-trending**
- **filter_list_24px** to **icon-filter**
- **expand_more_24px** to **icon-collapse**

Here's how the Layers panel for the icons should look now:

Now, anyone can see at a glance how to use the icons.

Documenting the filter and genre tags

Next, you'll work on the filter and genre tags. Visually, they're similar. Someone working with these components on another project or feature might accidentally use the wrong one. To help convey the components' intents, you'll add documentation that will show up in the **Assets** section.

Select the **Filter/Unchecked** component. A description field will show up on the Properties panel on the right:

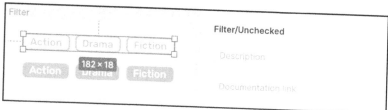

In the description field add "Filter criteria in selected state" for the selected state component. And add "Filter criteria in unselected state" for the unselected state component, as shown below.

Now, if you hover over the component in the **Asset** section, you'll notice a tooltip that gives more context about the component:

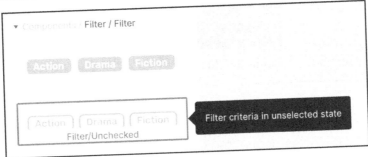

Next, add "Genre chips" to the documentation field for the genre component as well.

Your next goal is to look at how to standardize the buttons.

Converting buttons to components

As a final bit of cleanup for the project, you'll extract the buttons the prototype uses, convert them to components and use the components instead.

Start by creating a new frame measuring **422×221** on the Components page. Name this frame **Buttons**.

Now, head to the **Cinematic App Prototype** page and select the **Add to Watchlist** and **Mark Watched** buttons. Then, cut them (**Command/Control-X**) and paste them (**Command/Control-V**) into the **Buttons** frame.

Convert each of them into a component by using the **Create Component** option from the top toolbar.

Here's how your button's frame should look:

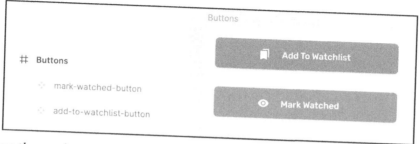

Now, use the newly created component in the **Cinematic App Prototype** and the main **Cinematic App** pages. Simply drag the relevant buttons into the frame, center them horizontally and place them at a margin of **32** from the bottom of the frame.

Now, to complete the design process, you'll look at how Figma takes care of developer handoff.

Handling code generation & asset exports

When building screens in code, developers target a multitude of device sizes and resolutions. This is difficult because they have to fit the same amount of information into a variety of screen sizes.

One of the things that's often a mundane, yet essential, part of the process is getting the correct assets and imagery for a specific resolution and device scale.

Figma makes it relatively straightforward to export assets, like icons, in varying resolutions. You can export any UI element from Figma, but in this case, you'll look at the icons.

Exporting icons

Go back into the **Components** page and select the icons from the **Icons** frame.

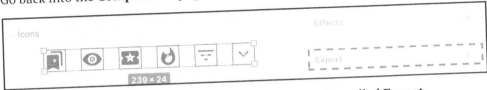

On the Properties panel on the right, you'll notice a section called **Export**.

Click the **+** button to add an export setting.

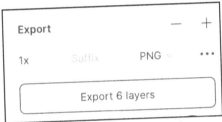

The export settings have three options:

- **Scale**: Defines how big or small the exported asset is. Use **x** as the suffix of a value to denote a multiplier, **h** for fixed height or **w** for fixed width.

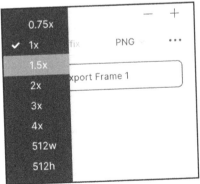

- **Suffix**: Denotes the scale at which you'll export the asset: @2x, @3x, etc.

- **Filetype**: The file format you'll use to export the asset: PNG, SVG, JPG, etc.

While developers who have access to the design file can configure the export settings and obtain the assets, you'll make their job easier by preconfiguring the settings as per their requirements:

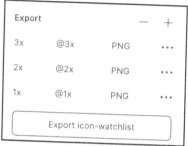

For Cinematic set the icons to **1x**, **2x**, and **3x** scales in the **PNG** format.

Generating code for UI elements

Another helpful feature from Figma is code generation for UI elements. Select any UI element, like components, shapes, frames or groups, and click the **Inspect** tab in the Properties panel on the right:

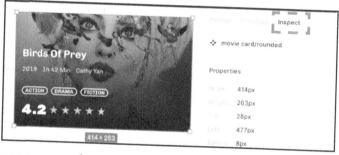

This will show you some reference UI code for the selected element:

Figma offers reference UI code for iOS, Android and the Web (CSS only). Note that the code isn't production-ready by any means. It only contains visual information like width, height, margins and spacing.

You'll often need to do some tweaking to make that code scale across device sizes. Nevertheless, it's a convenient way to quickly export the visual boilerplate when building the first version of the product in code.

Where to go from here?

Congratulations, with the tweaks and edits you made, your project is far more documented and flexible than before. Not only did you decompose your designs into their logical layers, but you also conveyed more information about lower-level details like colors and text styles.

Although the project you worked on targeted a relatively small app, the methods you learned up will scale along with the complexity of your projects.

Larger apps that offer more features will have more flows to think about, more iterations to perfect and more components to build.

They'll also have more moving pieces and conventions to follow that will change as you switch between projects and teams. Still, the process you work through will essentially boil down to the same fundamental methods you worked through in this book.

Before you wrap up this chapter, I'd like to point you to an extremely helpful resource that you can look to for inspiration and guidance when designing a new product. It's a publication called Design Systems (http://designsystems.com) from Figma that dives into each aspect of building a design system including colors, typography and iconography.

The best part about this publication is that it has a repo with design systems from popular products from GitHub, IBM, Zendesk and more publicly available for you to look at.

While not all of them are built on Figma, they offer a glimpse into how large organizations think about design and leverage their design systems. These examples show how a design system can effectively organize a company's design strategy, but also how different and unique design systems are.

Key points

- You learned about what design systems are.

- You covered the steps you took so far toward creating a design system.

- You improved the typography and colors section of the design system with helpful documentation.

- You explored Figma's assistive developer handoff features.

In the next chapter, you'll go over a quick recap of the book and learn about where to go next with the skills you've acquired.

Chapter 11: Recap & Next Steps

By Prateek Prasad

Over the course of the last ten chapters, you've gone from playing with basic shapes to building a full-fledged design system that acts as a foundation for your movie app. You learned about low-level design concepts like colors and typography and you built style guides for them. You realized the significance of flexibility and modularization in design and leveraged what you learned to build a component library to serve as a foundation for designing your app's screens.

This has been a long journey, and you've added many essential skills to help you in your journey as a designer. This new information will come in handy when working on a new project, helping you collaborate more effectively and empathetically with your design team.

Before finishing the book, take a moment for a quick recap of the previous chapters and to get some ideas about where to go next with your new-found skills.

Recapping the book

You'll now Look back over everything you learned. You can also use it in the future, to help you find the right chapter if you want to refresh your memory on a specific subject.

Chapter 1: Book Overview & App Preview

The book started with a quick introduction to design and its importance in building an inclusive and satisfying product. You set up your Figma account, then got a high-level overview of the app you'd build. You finished the chapter by adding some interactions to a prebuilt app prototype.

Chapter 2: Workspace Tour & Figma Fundamentals

Chapter 2 kicked off with a quick walkthrough of the Figma interface and some fundamental concepts to help you work with the tool. You played with basic shapes and styled them with fills, strokes, gradients, then learned about effects. You then covered layers and the alignment options available in Figma and used that information to build the sign-in screen for the app.

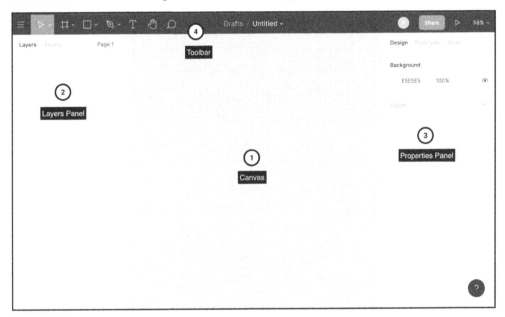

Chapter 3: App Teardowns

Chapter 3 took a slight detour to show you how to build an eye for good design. You learned how to boil screens down to their simplest building blocks and realized that most screens are built using just a handful of elements. It's the variation in placement and data that creates unique experiences. You compared how two popular apps, Airbnb and PocketCasts, leverage reusable components with variations in data to create drastically different experiences in their discovery screens.

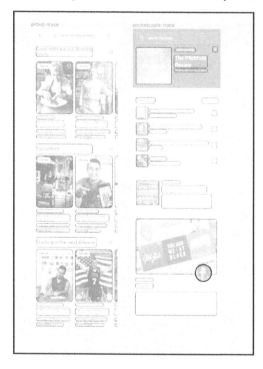

Chapter 4: Wireframing & Screen Layout

Chapter 4 introduced you to the concept of wireframing and its importance in a design cycle. You learned how to reduce the app's essence into key intents and components. You then used low fidelity wireframes to iterate on those intents. You got your first glimpse at the importance of reusability and built a component to create wireframes for the app's key screens.

Chapter 5: Reusable Elements & Data

In Chapter 5, you built on what you learned in the previous chapters to decompose your designs into small, flexible and reusable components. You then leveraged these components to build out your app's different screens. You also learned how to organize your designs using pages in Figma and how to use existing design libraries and plugins to make the design process easier.

Chapter 6: Typography

In Chapter 6, you dug deeper into the lower-level details of design, typography. You learned about the fundamentals of typography: fonts, typefaces and weights. You then used that information to build a typographic scale for your app and incorporate it into your app's design.

Rating

Title

Section Header

Button Text

Movie Info

Body Text

Navigation Text

User Rating Text

GENRE TEXT

Chapter 7: Colors

Chapter 7 continued with the lower-level details of design by diving into colors. You learned about the basics of color theory including what hue, saturation, contrast are and how they make designs more accessible. You then built the app's color styles and incorporated them into the design.

Triadic

Chapter 8: Transitions & App Flow

In Chapter 8, the app came to life with transitions. You played with the different transition and animation options available in Figma to build a fully interactive prototype. You created different screen destinations within the app and handled the various interaction states within the app.

Chapter 9: Feedback & Testing

In Chapter 9, you handed the designs to your team for feedback and testing. You learned about the collaboration features available in Figma and you incorporated the feedback left by various stakeholders, including a filter feature and a new iteration for the movie list UI.

Chapter 10: Design Systems

Finally, in Chapter 10, you learned about design systems and realized how everything you've done so far worked toward building a design system. You learned about the importance of documentation and improved your design system with helpful documentation. You finally looked at more elaborate and comprehensive design systems built for large scale projects.

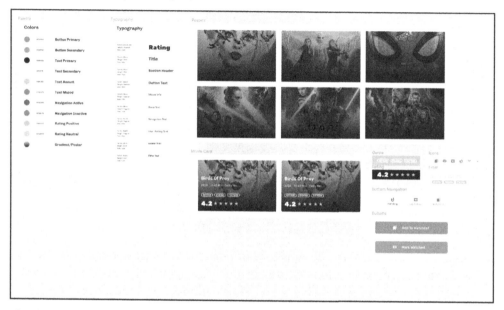

This brings you to this chapter. You've learned quite a lot, so take a step back to reflect upon how much you've grown throughout the last ten chapters. The skills you've picked up in this book will help you build inclusive products that look great.

Design is not just about the look and visual appeal of an app, but also about the emotions it invokes and how it simplifies a problem. Building something that looks great while being easy to understand and to adopt by a large audience is no easy job.

With the skills you've covered here, you'll be able to look deeper at problems in your app and ask questions to solve those problems at a more fundamental level.

More importantly, these skills give you the language to communicate and better collaborate with your design teams. You'll have more insight into their process and be able to contribute toward the ideation of the product. As an engineer, you can use your knowledge to identify constraints early on and bring your perspective to the process.

Where to go from here?

With your shiny new design skills, the world is your oyster. You can take on new projects and crank their polish up to 11. But, if you're keen on expanding these skills, I have a few recommendations for you:

- **"The Design of Everyday Things" by Don Norman**: Consider this the bible in the world of design, the book most designers swear by. This book takes examples from real-world objects, like doors and light switches, to uncover their usability issues and how you can build products that effortlessly guide their users to the correct actions.

- **"Thinking with Type" by Ellen Lupton**: This is a personal favorite because I'm a sucker for great typography. This book goes deep into typography and discusses aspects like font combination aesthetics. The best parts about this book are that it's exercise-oriented and it goes into the history of typography.

- **"Graphic Style: From Victorian to Hipster" by Steven Heller and Seymour Chwast**: This book is like a historical archive or a survey of different design styles spanning decades. It's full of illustrations and gives you an idea of how modern design is, in many ways, influenced by history and global cultures of the past.

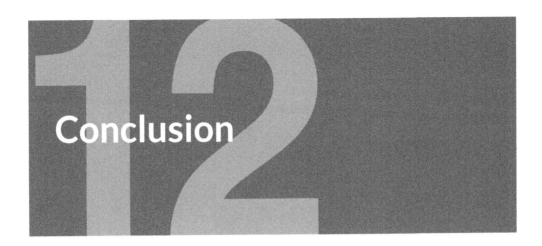

Conclusion

We hope this book has helped you add many essential design skills. You're well on your way to designing your own apps that work great, look even better, and are a delight to use.

The new information you have learned will come in handy when working on a new project, helping you collaborate more effectively and empathetically with your design team.

If you have any questions or comments as you work through this book, please stop by our forums at https://forums.raywenderlich.com and look for the particular forum category for this book.

Thank you again for purchasing this book. Your continued support is what makes the books, tutorials, videos and other things we do at raywenderlich.com possible. We truly appreciate it!

Happy designing!

- Prateek, Luke, Lea, Sandra, and Matthew

The *App Design Apprentice* team

Made in the USA
Columbia, SC
11 November 2021

48757182R00154